A
SKEPTIC'S
QUEST

A SKEPTIC'S QUEST

Josh McDowell's Search for Reality

BY JOE MUSSER

Here's Life Publishers, Inc.
San Bernardino, California 92402

A SKEPTIC'S QUEST
by Joe Musser

previously published in hardback as
JOSH: EXCITEMENT OF THE UNEXPECTED

Published by
HERE'S LIFE PUBLISHERS, INC.
P.O. Box 1576
San Bernardino, CA 92402

Library of Congress Catalogue Card 81-81210
ISBN 0-86605-151-1
HLP Product No. 403279

Printed in the United States of America.

This book is dedicated to Marvin
Palmquist, who—like Josh—is not
afraid to dream the impossible for God.

His unmistakable optimistic courage and
practical achievement is contagious.
Marv is a continuing source of in-
spiration and godly leadership.

—Joe Musser

LET'S STAY -IN- TOUCH!

If you have grown personally as a result of this material, we should stay in touch. You will want to continue in your Christian growth, and to help your faith become even stronger, our team is constantly developing new materials.

We are now publishing a monthly newsletter called 5 Minutes with Josh which will

1) tell you about those new materials as they become available
2) answer your tough questions
3) give creative tips on being an effective parent
4) let you know our ministry needs
5) keep you up to date on my speaking schedule (so you can pray).

If you would like to receive this publication, simply fill out the coupon below and send it in. By special arrangement 5 Minutes with Josh will come to you regularly — no charge.

Let's keep in touch!

Josh

☐ **Yes!** I want to receive the free subscription to **5 Minutes with JOSH**

_____
NAME

_____
ADDRESS

_____
CITY, STATE/ZIP

SLC-2024

Mail To:
Josh McDowell
c/o 5 Minutes with Josh
Campus Crusade for Christ
Arrowhead Springs
San Bernardino, CA 92414

This book is the account of an ordinary person endowed with extraordinary power because of his commitment to Jesus Christ.

That commitment helps explain why Josh McDowell has given more than 14 thousand messages to 7 million students and faculty at more than 600 universities in 60 countries. He has written 18 best-selling books and produced 47 cassette tapes, and he has been featured in 14 films and 2 television specials.

Our heavenly Father makes beautiful pottery from ordinary clay. Joe Musser would like to believe that the story of Josh's quest for truth will encourage you in your quest and that Josh's commitment to Christ will help you make your own commitment complete. As you read this stranger-than-fiction account from the pen of a master craftsman and wordsmith, we hope it will inspire you to trust God to use you in some special way to affect the lives of others.

We believe you will agree that *Joni* co-author Joe Musser has captured the excitement which characterizes the life of Josh McDowell—the excitement of an honest skeptic's discovery and sharing of God's truth.

—The Publisher

CHAPTER ONE

ELEVEN-YEAR-OLD JOSLIN MCDOWELL was pitching hay into the cow stalls in the old barn when he heard the noise. Auto horns and loud voices intruded in the usually tranquil farm surroundings.

He felt a twist in his stomach—the same scared-nauseous feeling he got when Mrs. Patten hollered at him for stuttering during recitation.

Young Josh didn't understand everything that was happening across the field at the house of his older brother Wilmot and his wife. Yet he knew it was something bad.

This was probably the single most important event to come into the life of the boy. He remembered the other time, a few days before his sixth birthday, when there was excitement like this. But that had been a celebration. His dad had called it V-J Day and it had something to do with the war.

People honked their horns then, too. But it was because they were happy—not angry. Josh was happy then because it meant his older sister, Shirley, an Army nurse stationed in Europe, would be coming home. He really loved Shirley. She was 23 years older than he was. In age, Shirley was more like his mother and Mom was more like a grandmother. Shirley always brought Josh something exciting and unique when she came home on furloughs. That was always a fun time of reunion—with lots of homemade ice cream and Mom's special homemade root beer.

Now the war was over and Shirley had been back for several years, and married. Wilmot had also married, and was living in a house Dad had built for him on the family's 2-acre dairy farm near Union City, Michigan.

JOSH

Josh stood the pitchfork against one of the stalls and kicked at the forkfull of hay he had missed. He both wanted to and didn't want to see what was going on at his brother's house.

His young mind wasn't able to grasp the significance of the event. He knew, however, it had caused a deep rift between Wilmot and his parents.

Josh walked slowly toward the farmhouse. His dad's pickup was gone, but Mom was inside. The old screen door had swollen bulges in the wire mesh from countless shoves of eager young hands as their owners ran in and out. It squeaked loudly when the boy went inside.

The sound alerted his mother who made a futile attempt to hide her tears in a dish towel. It was too late.

The young boy looked up at his mother helplessly. She knew his eyes were a mirror of her own. It was impossible to hide her hurt. She gathered the boy to her and all but smothered him in her ample middle.

"It's so awful," she sobbed, rocking with the boy. "It's the worst thing that could ever happen to anyone."

It must be a terrible thing, thought Josh, *even worse than when Aunt Liz died.* Josh had heard his brother and father argue but had no idea what the fights were about.

"Your brother is suing us for everything," his mother explained through her tears.

She explained how Wilmot had worked with Dad on the farm for some seven years and now felt he was entitled to half of it. "It's that woman he married," Mom said. "She's a possessive and domineering woman. Wilmot wouldn't act like that if she didn't put him up to it."

"But Mom," the boy said looking up at her, "I thought Dad gave Wilmot the new house and land by it for his own farm."

"Yes, he did," his mother admitted. "He gave him a house and would have been willing to give him half the farm, just as he asked for. Your father may have faults, but a lack of generosity isn't one of them."

"Huh?"

"I mean, your father don't always show it, but he's a loving man. He'd have given Wilmot what he wanted except for the way he came across. Wilmot *demanded* it—half of it.

*CHAPTER
ONE*

And when your dad said no, he hired himself a smart lawyer
and now he's *suing* us. The court says we have to pay him
and give him the new house. It's going to wipe us out and
probably kill your dad." The heavy woman began to cry
uncontrollably. Josh tried at first to console her, but when it
was obvious she was not responding, he gently pulled away
and went back outside.

Across the field the situation was at a point of
climax. The sheriff and a deputy had arrived with the court
order. They were accompanied by many of the families of
Union City, coming out in support of Wilmot against the
elder McDowell, and chanting words of encouragement to
Wilmot and his wife.

A construction crew had worked quickly, putting
the supports beneath the new house.

From a distance young Josh watched as the crew
jacked up the house to move it to a new lot. Wilmot was in
the yard digging up the small trees and shrubs his mother had
planted for the couple. Josh was glad his mother couldn't see
this. It was a strange event. Josh felt like crying because he
knew this embarrassment with the townspeople and the
separation of family was hurting his mother.

Yet, contrasted with this sensitivity were the aspects
of the situation itself. These he observed with an objectivity
that placed the happenings in a neutral setting. In fact, it was
this part of him that wanted to go up there and watch. He
wondered about the moving company; how it was possible to
move a house with a truck. He had never heard of anyone
taking a house and moving it somewhere else. That really
fascinated the young boy.

The family was affected in many ways by the actions of the oldest brother. Probably the most serious were
not the financial aspects, however. They had to sell the family
cottage on the lake and make other belt-tightening changes.
Yet, these were not as difficult as Mom had predicted. The
emotional results were far more damaging. There was a deep,
bloody wound left that simply refused to heal. Josh thought
of the times his father had killed chickens for Sunday dinner.
He'd place a small hard stick or scrap of wood on the
chicken's neck, holding the head to the ground. Then, he
would separate the head from the body by pulling the bird,

JOSH

and drop the chicken into the grass to flap itself dead. That was the image he now had of the family—as though one part had been physically pulled from the other—eventually killing both parts.

For the most part, however, Josh McDowell was a happy youngster. He grew up on the farm Aunt Liz had given to his father and mother. It sometimes seemed strange to him that he had two older sisters and a brother—all old enough to be his parents—and that he and brother Jim were more than 20 years younger.

Jim and Josh were the only ones left at home now. Both boys helped with the chores, but Jim had been looking for a job. When he found a job, with a neighboring farmer, Josh took up the slack by doing his chores, too. It was his responsibility to help twice a day with the milking, shovel manure from the barn, and feed the calves each day.

In school Josh did well. But he had a stutter which seemed to show up mainly in class. His second grade teacher, Mrs. Duel, in her zeal to change Josh from being left-handed to right-handed, no doubt started it. Josh was supposed to build imaginary houses with wooden blocks on the play table. Every time he reached for a block with his left hand, Mrs. Duel smacked the table—and sometimes his hand—with her yardstick.

"Think, Josh, *think*," she'd yell at him, "you're doing it *wrong!* Think! Do it with your right hand!"

In third grade, things were the same. "Use your other hand," his teacher told him again and again. When the frustration made the boy stutter, the teachers got after him for that, too. "Think, Josh. Don't stutter. *Concentrate!*" That only made it worse.

When Josh was in the fifth grade, he was asked to recite the Gettysburg Address, and it made him sick. Waves of nausea washed over him when he heard Mr. Wade call on him. It wasn't because he hadn't done his homework. At home, feeding the cows, he could recite it brilliantly. But now it was awful.

"Stop stuttering and say it!" Mr. Wade ordered. Josh could hear the giggles and snickers. "F-four...four-sc-scor...uh..." More giggles.

"I c-can't d-do it!" Josh shouted and ran from the room.

*CHAPTER
ONE*

No one had told Josh that what they were trying to do was for his ultimate benefit, since society favored right-handedness.

Eventually, Josh learned to compensate. He found that by striving harder than others, he could please teachers and parents with his work. He was soon getting the highest grades in class and excelling in sports.

Once every year a certain man and woman came to his school. They told flannelgraph stories and handed out little red New Testaments. They called themselves *Gideons,* and Josh enjoyed their stories—at least in the earlier years. Later, when the boys from seventh and eighth grades gathered behind the gas station to smoke, he heard some of them mocking the Gideons and their Scriptures.

He tried one of their milder jokes on his brother that night. "Hey, Jim—what's black and white and red all over?"

"That's easy—a newspaper," Jim sniffed.

"Then, what's black and blue and red all over?" Josh grinned.

"I dunno, what?"

"A holy roller readin' a Bible and fallin' down the stairs."

Both boys chuckled. But their mother looked up quickly from her chair, glaring at them. "Don't you *ever* let me hear you mock the Bible or God again! You're supposed to know better. Didn't I bring you up to respect God and religion?"

"Yes, Ma'am," the boys replied in repentant unison.

She *had* instilled a respect for church and God in the boys. She even drove them in the pickup to town on Sunday morning and dropped them off for Sunday school and church.

Josh's mother was a big woman. Not tall, but quite stout. She often hugged Josh when he was a small boy and joked about how he couldn't get his small arms around her. Or she'd hold on to him and laugh as they tried—unsuccessfully—to go through a doorway sideways.

It was her great size which also made Josh glad that *she* was the family disciplinarian and not his dad. Mom would try to spank the boy when it was necessary, but often found it hard to hold the squirming youngster, chase him around the table and apply the licks from the belt at the same time. As long as Josh screamed and cried—often with make-believe tears—the punishment seemed complete.

But as much as Josh loved his mother, he hated her husband, his father. Basically, his dad was a good man—when he wasn't drinking. Those times were rare, however. It seemed to Josh his dad was always drunk—or recovering.

Many times the old man had embarrassed Josh because of his drinking.

The boy wasn't really conscious that his hatred for his father's drinking had turned into hatred for his father himself. At one end-of-the-year school outing, the class voted to have a picnic at the McDowell farm. Everyone was having a good time until his father drove into the driveway lane. The old pickup weaved back and forth, kicking up clouds of dust as Dad drove toward the barn. He had barely avoided hitting a tree, a fence and Josh's pet collie.

As the man stopped the pickup and got out, he nearly fell, then staggered toward the house. When the kids saw he was intoxicated, they laughed and joked. Josh ran to the barn, too ashamed, too embarrassed to be with them.

Josh hated his father for the embarrassment and shame his alcoholism caused the family. He also resented what it caused his father to do to his mother.

On several occasions Josh had come out to the barn to find his mother, sprawled in the manure gutter of the cow stalls, weeping and bruised from being shoved and hit by his father.

She was a patient woman and put up with a great deal of abuse. But even she had her limits. Twice she left home. The first time was when Josh was 12. He found a note for his father when he came home from school one day:

I'm going to Chicago to find work. When I get settled, I'll send for Jim and Josh to live with me.

Josh was quite upset at that turn of events. It was several days before his mother called to say she was all right in Chicago, and had found work as a chauffeur for a city couple too old to drive.

However, after much pleading and promises from her husband and a visit in Chicago by Shirley, Mom came home.

One other time she left for a couple of weeks, then returned. She seemed to be marking time, however. It was almost as if she had a future agenda in mind and was content to go through the motions of life until then.

As a growing junior high boy, Josh was developing intellectually and physically. Neither of his parents had more than a grade school education, but he was determined to better himself. His older brother, Jim, was planning to go to the state university and do something with his life, too. Josh also looked forward to leaving the farm and going to college. Since the lawsuit over Wilmot's claim to half the farm and the new house, the family had no finances to send the younger boys to college. But both resolved to pay their own expenses.

College was a goal, a dream. Not so much in terms of achievement that advanced education meant. Rather, it was a ticket to something better—a way to leave the small town. But it would be several years before Josh was old enough to leave the farm.

Josh thought of the Wilson family. They fit his idea of a success. Mr. Wilson was a well-to-do industrialist from Detroit. His son worked summers on the farm. "Sonny" was five years older and, Josh thought, infinitely wiser. The Wilson family used the McDowell farm as a "summer house." They stayed there as guests. Mom fixed them meals, took care of their rooms, and generally made them feel comfortable enough to want to return for the five or seven summers they stayed.

The Wilsons' coming fueled Josh's desire to leave home and be a success. Sometimes his desire was so strong he thought of running away and starting out on his own.

That ran against the grain of his upbringing, however. His mother's instruction and example was a strong deterrent to such a foolish and impetuous act. So was his father's influence.

JOSH

Despite his hatred for his father, he was grateful for the sense of responsibility the man had instilled in him. Although his dad drank hard, he also worked hard. He taught Josh that you worked hard to earn your bread and board, and you did every job right.

His father was a good worker, and were it not for alcohol, would have been highly successful. In fact, he had tasted success and lost it. In earlier years he had been the manager of a large A & P food store in Detroit. Because of his drinking, he was demoted to the job of manager of a small local A & P in Union City. He lost that job, too. That's when Aunt Liz, from Philadelphia, had compassion on the couple and gave both of them the farm in Union City.

The work of running a dairy farm required long hours and manpower of more than casual commitment. His dad, by the example of his work, demonstrated to the boy a deep sense of responsibility. Even in financial matters he trained Josh well. He was taught to spend his earnings wisely and save for those things he wanted. When something was beyond his immediate ability to pay, such as a new bike (and later his first car), the elder McDowell did not give his son the money. Instead he took him to the Union City Bank and co-signed a loan with the boy. Josh learned that the loan was his responsibility and he would have to pay it back in regular installments. This gave him a real sense of satisfaction and pride. Also, because his possessions were so hard to come by, he gave them greater care.

These momentary times of respect for his father were all too few, however. Josh joined the Boy Scouts and spent much of his free time in sports to overcome this lack of relationship with his father. But the athletic trophies and scouting honors merely stood on the shelves in his room. They gave no lasting satisfaction nor did they add anything to his life in any real way.

In order to keep his shame, anger and embarrassment to a minimum, Josh often resorted to extreme means. If his father was drunk and threatening to physically abuse his mother, or if he was merely in the way when friends were to call, Josh would drag the older man to the barn and tie him to a stall to sleep off a stupor.

As he grew older, and bolder, he did this more

CHAPTER
ONE

often. Also, he became more brutal, tying his father so that his feet were trussed with a rope that was noosed around his neck. The boy hoped his father would kick his legs trying to get free and choke himself.

Other grim and difficult memories persist. On one occasion Josh flew into a rage at his father and tried to sober him up by shoving him, fully dressed, into the bathtub. A struggle ensued, and Josh found himself holding his dad's head under water, nearly drowning him.

Fortunately, someone intervened just in time, surprised that the 14-year-old boy had both the strength and motivation to take his father's life.

It was difficult for both parents and youngster to deal with such unusual moments. By the time his dad had sobered up, the matter was usually swept under the rug to be forgotten. Later such incidents were neither discussed nor dealt with.

One day when his father was away, Josh decided to teach himself how to drive. He climbed into the pickup truck followed by his big collie, and they shared the front seat. He turned on the ignition and pushed in the clutch pedal as he had so often seen his dad do. He pushed the gearshift down as he let up on the clutch and heard a grinding sound as the gears somehow meshed. The pickup lurched forward down the lane as Josh next jerked it into second gear.

It took several trips back and forth on the long drive between the barn and the road before Josh mastered shifting. His dog barked excitedly as the truck bounced crazily down the lane. When he successfully learned how to shift, Josh tried his hand at racking and braking the pickup. There was a cloud of dust and the noisy whine of differential gears as the truck neared 40 miles an hour in second gear. Thoroughly excited, the big collie jumped into her master's lap, landed in a sprawl across Josh's chest and the steering wheel.

"Hey—get down!" he yelled. But not before the pickup grazed a huge oak, glanced off another tree trunk, mowed down several honeysuckle bushes, crashed through the white rail fence, and demolished the corner post at the end of the lane.

Finally stopped, Josh climbed out to check the damage. Not only had the truck destroyed everything in its path, but in so doing had completely crumpled a fender, bent the front bumper, broke a headlight and scarred the paint all along one side.

Josh felt sick. He picked up the corner post, and tried to stick it back into its hole. It leaned sadly to one side.

Quickly he climbed back into the pickup, drove it hurriedly back to the barn and parked it. Then he ran into the house and—at four o'clock in the afternoon—decided it was time to go to bed.

At five-thirty he heard both the screen door slam and the voice he had been awaiting with dread.

"Josh...where are you?" his dad called.

The youngster was afraid to answer. Finally a head poked inside his room. "Josh!" the man yelled. The boy sat bolt upright, trembling.

"Why aren't you out there feeding the calves like you're supposed to do?" There was no reference to the truck—yet, how could he have missed it?

Josh ran outside to do his chores. He lay awake all that night waiting for his father to come after him for what he did to the pickup. Nothing happened.

The next morning, after chores, Josh was leaving for school when he heard metallic noises coming from the shed. Josh peered inside and saw his father working on the crumpled fender and bumper, trying to pound out the dents.

It seemed apparent that his father thought *he* had wrecked the pickup while drunk and couldn't remember.

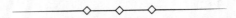

In high school, Josh himself learned how to repair cars. In auto shop, he began with the other boys to learn about brake master cylinders and valve grinding. He became skilled in repairing cars—so much so that he bought old "clunkers" and took them to auto shop class to fix up and sell. Each one he repaired he sold at a profit. Soon he had a car of his own.

CHAPTER
ONE

And with the car came a girl friend. He and Sharon were steadies throughout high school. They went together to the games and dances, enjoyed hamburgers and root beers almost nightly at the A & W stand. On Halloween Josh and his friends dumped over the outhouse of a local farmer. Despite a reward of $100 for information leading to those who did it, the farmer never learned that his own daughter was among those in the group who participated.

Sharon was fun to be with and Josh appreciated the fact that she—like him—preferred not to participate in the wilder parties where, more often than not, liquor was served.

Because of his father's example, Josh avoided these as well as the "six-pack busts" that some of the school ball players and others held regularly. It was no big deal to Josh that he shunned alcohol. But his mother was grateful.

Josh returned home from a date about midnight near the end of his senior year. He found his mother crying bitterly. (After one such previous episode where he found his mother crying, he took on his drunken father, wrestling him into the bathroom where he tried to stick his head in the toilet, pushing it up and down in the water. If the bowl had been deeper and he hadn't splashed most of the water out onto the floor, Josh probably would have drowned him.) So, although he often saw Mom crying, he had not seen her cry so hard since the day his brother sued his parents.

"Mom...what's the matter?" Josh asked gently.

It was several minutes before she had enough composure to answer. "It's all too much. I...I can't take it any more. Your...your father—" she wept, the words and sobs hard to separate. "His drinking...the abuse..." Josh swallowed, moved by her grief.

"I know, Mom..." Even Josh's strong-arm tactics with his father had not kept him from drinking.

"I can't take it any more. I...I want to wait until you're on your own after graduation next month—" she sobbed, "—then I just want to die."

It unnerved Josh to hear his mother talk that way. She often referred to herself in a self-deprecating manner, but he had never seen her quite this serious before, and it frightened him.

Some time later she called Josh into her room. His

JOSH

brother was away at the university and he knew his father was at the tavern in town. Dad never said that's where he was going when he left, of course. He always said simply, "I'm going to town—be back later." Yet, there was no question in anyone's mind where he could be found. The big farmhouse seemed particularly empty and quiet this night. Perhaps that is why, when his mother called him into her room, the act had a special significance.

"I want you to promise me three things," she said without preamble. "I want you to promise you'll never be an alcoholic, that you won't swear, and that you'll be the type of son I can be proud of."

Josh smiled at his mother. She had undoubtedly rehearsed this request in her own mind many times before saying it. It was said with the simplicity of someone reciting a shopping list. But its importance was not easily dismissed by Josh. He gave her words the respect and consideration she wanted. He paused to think about what she had asked, then nodded with certainty. She took his response to be a promise, a vow—and returned his smile.

Josh looked into his mother's tired eyes. He was shocked to see how old she seemed to be getting. His feelings welled up deep inside. In a way it embarrassed him to feel the catch in his throat and have his eyes moisten—maybe such feelings were unmanly. Josh took a deep breath and put his hand on her shoulder.

"I promise, Mom," he added. "I promise to be the kinda son you'll be proud of."

Once again he felt the catch in his throat. How vulnerable she looked. His mind went back to what seemed just a few years. Was it possible for her to age so much in that time? He remembered her stout body as robust; now it was tired, swollen. In recent years she had come to be ashamed of her appearance. When she took the boys to high school games, she always sat in the car because she didn't want to meet people. Josh had always figured it was because she was ashamed of his father.

A strange imperceptible quality was present in the house after the night Josh found his mother crying. Although he wasn't consciously aware of it, his mother had lost the will to live.

CHAPTER TWO

JOSH

JOSH GRADUATED FROM HIGH SCHOOL IN MAY, 1957. About that same time, because it was the thing to do, he enlisted in the Air National Guard with several high school buddies. He went to Guard training one weekend a month and was scheduled for two weeks of active duty training at a military base each summer.

He planned these around the summer job he landed at a factory in Battle Creek. Josh went to work on the assembly line, but, except for the good pay, didn't like it.

"It's boring," he complained to his foreman one day.

"Well kid," the foreman laughed, "welcome to the real world. You high school kids think the world owes you some glamorous, exciting job?"

"No sir," Josh replied. "But what's the best-paying job in the plant?"

"Best paying? I suppose welding, why? I thought you were bored. Welding ain't any less boring than what you're doin' now."

"Maybe so. But if I'm gonna be bored, I might as well make the most money doin' it," Josh grinned.

"What makes you think you could get a job welding?" the foreman asked.

"I was hopin' you'd get it for me. I can weld. I know how. I did it in auto shop at school."

"Uh-huh," the foreman nodded. "But what they do here makes that seem like playin' with Tinker Toys. C'mon, get back on line now. Do your dreamin' on your own time."

"But I want to be a welder."

"No. You *can't*. Now, get back to work."

JOSH

Reluctantly Josh walked back to the assembly line. His mind, not required for the task at hand, was free to concoct plans and create schemes. So, at the next break period he went to the inter-office phone and looked up the extension number of the shop superintendent.

"Mr. Burke?" Josh asked in his oldest, most mature-sounding voice.

"Yes," the man answered.

"I understand you need good welders."

"Uh...yeah, why?"

"Well, you've got probably the best welder in Battle Creek right here in the shop but he's working on the assembly line. You ought to transfer him," Josh suggested.

"Oh yeah?" Burke replied. "Who is it?"

"Name's McDowell. Josh McDowell."

"Send him to my office in the morning. I'll talk to him," Burke told him and hung up.

Grinning widely, Josh replaced the phone on its cradle and whistling, swaggered back to the assembly line.

The next morning Josh reported to Mr. Burke. He was brief and spent only a few minutes interviewing Josh. Then he turned Josh over to one of his veteran welders, a muscular black man.

"Charlie, take him to the welding area and give him the standard welding test," Burke told the black man, who nodded and indicated with outstretched thumb where that would be.

In the welding area Josh paused to look at the finished pieces stacked to be moved.

"Who did this welding work?" Josh asked.

"I did—why?" Charlie replied.

"Well, it's better than any work I've ever seen. There's no way I could get a seam that smooth and even—to begin with. I might not even pass your welding test. How about it, man? Can you give me a break? I can weld—and I learn fast."

The other man smiled. "Okay...let's see what you can do now. I'll see if you know enough about welding so's I can teach you how we do it here."

Josh proved to be a fast study. He learned quickly and was soon turning out work as good as that of his mentor.

CHAPTER
TWO

In fact, because the task was as routine as the assembly line assignment, once again his mind began to work. He conceived a jig which would hold the piece to be welded. It was his own invention to streamline the process. Using it meant he could turn out more work. But such productivity, he soon learned, was frowned upon by both management and labor. The unions didn't like it because it meant more work could be done by fewer people. Thus, jobs might be eliminated. The bosses didn't like it because the unions didn't—and peace with the union was more essential than increased productivity.

On the night shift, Josh was turning out 30 welded units instead of the designated 12. The union wanted him fired. The foreman struck a deal.

Josh would be allowed to use his invention and turn out 30 units a night. But they would only record 12 units. The extras would be put in a "bank." That way he could come to work and punch in for *several weeks,* but didn't have to do anything. He could read, sleep, study—whatever he wanted—except welding.

Jim came home from the university and seemed to Josh to be a different person. He seemed all grown up—self-confident, suave and brilliant.

"I di'n't think there was so much differences in high school and college," Josh observed.

"Oh, Josh—your grammar and pronunciations are *awful,"* Jim said. "First of all, it's *did*n't—not *di'n't.* Then you've mixed singular and plural cases. You should say, 'I *didn't* think there *were* so *many* differences in high school and college."

Josh looked at his older brother. "Hey, get off my case, huh? You think I'm still in school?"

"Sorry," Jim shrugged. "Just trying to help. I sounded just like you when I went off to college and they treated me like a 'hick.' You should work on your grammar and punctuation before you go."

"First things first. I gotta go to Guard camp this summer first."

"*Have* to, not gotta," Jim corrected.

JOSH

Actually Josh was looking forward to the active training stint with his buddies. Instead of going to the Battle Creek armory for drill, they'd get to go to a real Air Force Base somewhere in the U.S. But in true military fashion, Josh's orders were not with those of his friends when they received notification to report to Lackland Air Force Base near San Antonio.

He complained to the captain who merely shrugged. "It happens. You might get orders to go later. Then again, they could send you somewhere else. Or, you might get passed over completely. It sometimes happens with the orders of first-timers."

"But I want to go with my buddies," Josh complained.

"Sorry," the captain replied.

"Come on, sir. Please."

"I said I'm sorry," the captain repeated. "It's impossible. It *can't* be done."

"Don't say *can't* to me, sir," Josh said. "I don't believe in the word 'can't.'"

The captain sat back in the ancient wooden swivel chair and smiled. But he still shook his head at the young man's request.

Josh knew that there is always a way. However, sometimes emotions obscure logic and intelligence. In order to join Marv Mulligan and his other buddies in San Antonio, Josh found a way. By enlisting in the regular Air Force for a four-year active duty stint, he'd be able to be with them in basic training at Lackland Air Force Base.

The questionable wisdom of such a decision was uppermost in his mind as he now stood before the recruiter, his arm upraised, taking the oath of service and allegiance to his country.

McDowell, he thought as he stood there, *are you sure you want to do this? Four years is a long time.*

CHAPTER THREE

After two weeks of active duty training at Lackland Air Force Base, Marv Mulligan and his buddies went home to Michigan. Airman Josh McDowell, however, stayed behind. As a recruit, he still had over ten weeks of basic training left.

That he had made a mistake was to totally understate the situation. However, once in, Josh determined to make the most of it.

He was assigned to the "05" squadron, an extra-disciplined recruit training unit. It was part of a new Air Force program designed to instill confidence, discipline and self-reliance. The program appealed to Josh, who went to the director of his unit one day.

"I'd like the job of unit leader," he said.

His superior, a grizzled master sergeant with more than two decades of service, looked up from his desk.

"Why?" he asked Josh coldly.

"I think I have what it takes. And I'd like to work on improving myself," he replied.

"You're a cocky s.o.b., aren't you?"

Josh seemed honestly surprised. "No...I don't mean it that way. I really would like to try it."

The older man ran a huge paw over his nearly-shaved head and pursed his lips. His eyes narrowed as he seemed to try and read Josh's thoughts. Then he nodded slowly.

"We'll see if you've got the right stuff. I'll give you a crack at it."

Josh approached the job of unit leader with even more energy and discipline than the experienced noncommissioned military men. He had his recruits up earlier than the other platoons. When the others marched to the mess hall, his men did it double-time. When the other platoons were called out for roll call, his men did calisthenics. There was resentment, of course, but it was tempered with pride. The recruits in Josh McDowell's platoon were the best on base, and everyone knew it. Occasionally Josh was carried away with his new sense of power. He would casually assign extra duty for what he felt was an infraction of procedure or policy. This assignment was sometimes arbitrary and unfair.

One recruit in particular annoyed Josh. He was a teenager from Pennsylvania, no older than Josh. He had a habit of getting up early to read his Bible and pray. Somehow such activities seemed out of place here, Josh thought. But instead of saying anything directly to the recruit, Josh eliminated his "extra" time for prayer by giving him more work details. He assigned "the preacher," as he was nicknamed, to KP and latrine detail with such regularity that it became obvious that Josh was picking on him.

On one occasion—after completing over 20 straight hours of KP—the young recruit went to the corner of the barracks where Josh bunked. He took the boots of his unit leader and gave them a superb shine.

The young man's Christian convictions were obviously more than just show. Josh took "Preacher" off further work details.

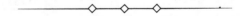

Josh had decided as long as the Air Force promised career training skills for its personnel, he would pursue technical training in some mechanical area for which he had aptitude. Such acquired skills and experience would help him find good work once he was discharged—although that event seemed far away just now. He applied for automotive repair training. The Air Force assigned him to the military police.

Josh went to talk to his training sergeant.

"I don't want to be in the MP's," he explained. "That's not even *close* to my interests."

"Oh yeah?" the sergeant asked in mock surprise. "Do you mean the Air Force made a mistake?"

"Uh...well, yes. I wanted to be assigned to

something mechanical. Can't I get assigned to something else?"

"Like what?"

"Well, what is there that's mechanical?"

"The only thing where I've got an opening is engine repairs."

"That's what I want!" Josh exclaimed.

"It's not what you think. It's airplane engines. Jet fighter planes."

"That's okay; an engine's an engine. I can take a car engine apart and fix it—I'll learn about jet planes," Josh replied.

"No, you can't."

"What do you mean, I can't?"

"That assignment calls for somebody with stripes. O.J.T."

"What's O.J.T.?" Josh asked.

"On the job training. There's two years of training, then a test to take after that. Only those who pass the test qualify."

"Is it possible to take the test without the two years of O.J.T.?"

"I suppose so. But it wouldn't do you any good. Everything you learn in those two years is in that test. Anybody who took it without the training would be wasting his time."

"When can I take the test?"

"Didn't you hear what I just said?" the sergeant asked.

"Yes. You said it was possible to take the test without the O.J.T. That's what I want to do."

"But you didn't hear the rest of it. You'd be wasting your time. It's all about jet engines. What you know about jet engines I can scribble on one sheet of toilet paper," the sergeant said sarcastically.

Josh only grinned. "When? When can I take the test?"

The other man sighed. "After you finish basic. You've got four and a half weeks."

Josh went into San Antonio on the weekend and got to the library before it closed. He checked out an armload of books on jet engines and headed back to the base. He tracked down as many manuals and technical books as he could find on the subject from the base library and began to study.

That was the impossible part. He was still in basic training and was engaged in that activity from dawn to dusk. Often he pulled extra duty which took away even more precious time.

What available time he had for study was concentrated between ten at night and sunrise. Since "lights out" was strictly enforced in the barracks, Josh retired to a laundry room in the basement of the building.

He taped cardboard over the window to maintain "lights out." He studied every available free hour over the next several weeks. He memorized everything to do with jet engines, their operation and repair.

The test was given to Josh as he had asked. He nervously awaited the results.

"You need an 85% score to pass," his training sergeant had warned him. "That's pretty tough even for those guys who have had two years of O.J.T. in the subject."

The test scores were returned. Airman McDowell had scored 86%. He was jubilant. His training sergeant merely shook his head in disbelief.

Basic training ended in the fall. The Air Force lost his orders, however, and Josh was stranded in limbo. Others went off to train at other bases. He and two other recruits, whose orders also were lost, stayed in San Antonio. With nothing to do but wait for the orders to catch up with them, they sat around—reporting as necessary to the duty sergeant— but going into town to roam and party the rest of the time.

They slept in the otherwise empty barracks, and finally not even the duty sergeant bothered them.

For two months they played and partied. Then the Air Force "found" them and their lost orders caught up. The three were shipped to Dover Air Force Base in Delaware.

But even here things were not all that serious. Josh was assigned to a unit that maintained C-133 aircraft—giant cargo planes the size of a modern jumbo jet. Seldom did Josh work on planes, however.

Because of his athletic ability, he was picked to be on the base basketball team. Such an honor reflected

CHAPTER
THREE

favorably on his unit, so his platoon leader treated him
royally. Josh enjoyed traveling with the base team in competition with teams from other air bases along the eastern
seaboard, including Bermuda.

However, he was also expected to pull some duty.
Sometimes he worked in the giant hangars where the C-133's
were kept. One day, while walking next to the scaffold where
a couple of airmen were working on an engine, he heard
someone yell.

Josh looked up just in time to see a big exhaust
pipe, slipping from the hands of a worker some 12 feet above
him. There was no time to react. The heavy pipe caught him
squarely across the head. He fell in a crumpled heap under
the pipe.

Josh woke up in a naval hospital in Philadelphia.
He did not remember much about the accident. He had
passed out the day after being hit in the head so they brought
him here.

The medical people weren't too helpful at first. He
tried to find out what was wrong, but they insisted on a
number of tests before making any commitments or
diagnoses.

Finally a doctor told him he had *cerebral verebras*
damage to the right side of his head. Since the brain was
affected, the hospital people decided to keep him there for
observation.

"How long?" Josh asked.

"I don't know. We'll take it a day at a time," the
doctor answered.

Some days later—on Friday, the 13th—Josh was
still recovering from his head injury in the hospital. He
looked up to see an Air Force officer enter the room.

Military personnel often came by, but this one
seemed different. He was hesitant and stood just inside the
door, as if unwilling to intrude.

The officer nervously turned his hat around and
around in his hands and finally cleared his throat, moving
forward a step or two.

"Uh...are you Airman McDowell?"

"Yessir."

The man's blue uniform seemed out of place with the hospital whites, but that isn't what made his visit seem strange. Josh frowned and raised his head. "What is it?"

"I...I'm Chaplain Purlman," the officer explained. "I'm afraid I have to give you some bad news."

"What is it?" Josh repeated. This time the question had an urgency.

"It's your mother," he replied simply. "Your mother just died."

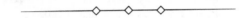

Lying in his hospital bed, Josh recalled his mother's statement four months earlier that she was waiting for his graduation, then "I just want to die."

It was too easy for Josh to blame his father for her death. The facts worked against his emotions.

"It was obvious your father loved her very much," Dr. Funk told Josh before the funeral. "He was by her side every night from six o'clock until six the next morning. He never slept. You could see him sharing her agony. Whatever pain your mother had, he had—in a deep spiritual sense. He loved her very much."

"Why did she die, doctor?" Josh asked. "I didn't know she was sick."

The doctor paused momentarily then said, "She was terribly sick. I was afraid of internal hemorrhage. That's why I stationed a nurse there during the day and your father was with her all night. If something happened, they'd be able to call a doctor right away."

"And—?"

"Well, on the third day..." the doctor seemed to hesitate. "One of the nurses left your mother to make a phone call. She was gone about eight or ten minutes. But in that time, your mother had an internal hemorrhage and died."

Josh's eyes filled with tears as they had done so many times since the chaplain first brought the news.

"Josh, there's such an irony in all this," Dr. Funk said, his voice tinged with anger and regret. "I was right in

CHAPTER
THREE

the next room. I could have *saved her*. I was right in the next room."

There were so many people to accuse for his mother's death—none really deserving blame. Yet, Josh vented his emotions and grief at his father, the nurse, the hospital—even himself, for whatever vague reasons. Logically, though, when he had time and distance to reflect, he realized she died—probably as much as anything—because she simply gave up; she just let go of life.

True to Josh's military experience, the period for his medical observation lasted several months. "Observation" meant that he was to be in the hospital from eight to five every day. But at night he was free to go out if he wanted. As a result, Josh dated a number of nurses and passed the time with frequent visits back to the Air Force base in Dover to see his buddies and Sgt. York, his company master sergeant.

It was winter when Josh was finally released from the hospital. The head injury had healed and seemingly hadn't resulted in any serious complications—except for one unsettling side effect.

There were times when Josh experienced memory lapses, periodic episodes of amnesia. Several times he'd find himself in downtown Dover, miles from the base, having absolutely no idea how he got there, or how long he'd been gone.

Another time, Josh woke up in his own bed in Union City, Michigan. Immediately he began to shake with fear, having no recollection of leaving Dover and traveling the several hundred miles across five states to get home.

"H-how'd I get here?" he asked his father somewhat sheepishly.

"Don't you remember?" his father smiled. "You hitchhiked. Came in last night. Don't remember, huh?" The old man winked, "I know how you feel."

"I haven't been drinking," Josh explained. "But my mind is completely blank about coming."

He reached for the telephone and called the base, asking for Sgt. York. After letting Josh explain his situation and why he was absent without leave, the voice on the phone laughed. "No problem, McDowell. Just get back here as soon as possible. I'll cover for you."

Josh hung up the telephone, still shaken. For the first time in his life he felt that he wasn't in complete control, and that bothered him greatly.

Sgt. York kidded him when he got back to Dover. "I never tried that amnesia bit on my C.O. That's a pretty good line."

"Except it isn't a line," Josh said soberly. "It really happened. And, Sarge—it scared me to death."

"Well, you got smacked on the head pretty good. It's a wonder you ain't dead."

"Yeah," replied Josh. "I guess I'm lucky when you look at it that way."

Josh's amnesia, his own close brush with death, and the experience of his mother's dying served to fuel long hours of serious introspection on Josh's part.

That weekend, he drove to Philadelphia and decided, on the spur of the moment, to go to church. He located a small Baptist church and went in and sat near the back.

Josh listened to an emotional sermon and watched as several people walked forward when the minister invited them to "accept Christ." The phrase was new and awkward to Josh. He had heard it before, but didn't know exactly what it meant.

Having attended, rather regularly, a traditional mainline Protestant church all his life, he felt he should have understood. Yet there seemed to be some hidden meaning to some of the terms the minister used.

Josh went back to the church the following weekend. This time, after the message, when the minister asked for those who wanted to "accept Christ" to go forward, Josh slowly rose from his seat and walked to the front.

Maybe there's something I've been missing in my religion, he thought. *These people seem to have something I don't have. But what is it?*

"Welcome, son. Glad to see you," a smiling man said quietly to Josh, extending his hand. "I'm Sam Markum, a deacon here. Let's kneel down and pray."

Josh felt conspicuous. He was not only in his

CHAPTER
THREE

uniform, but at the front of the church on his knees. He flushed self-consciously, feeling the stares of the people.

"Lord Jesus," the deacon prayed, "we thank Thee for Thy free gift of salvation. We thank Thee for Thy propitiation of our sins. And we thank Thee that this young man desires salvation. We thank Thee in Jesus' name, Amen."

Josh had kneeled and listened to the man's prayer. He understood practically none of it. He expected something to happen. Nothing did.

Nervously the deacon stood. "Uh...is there anything else I can do?"

"Well...I guess not," Josh replied. "Thanks."

And he left the church—with more confusion and questions than when he came.

The confusion gave way to frustration, the frustration turned to anger.

So that's religion! he thought. *A big zero—nothing.* What a letdown. Religion, he now saw, was an empty sham— rituals which had absolutely no effect on anything. He decided not to go back to the church.

CHAPTER FOUR

MASTER SERGEANT YORK, A CAREER AIR FORCE MAN, had become more than Josh's superior non-com. He was a friend. When Sgt. York suffered a heart attack in March, Josh came to visit him in the hospital every day—as soon as he was able to receive visitors.

"You're the only one to come and see me, McDowell," Sgt. York said.

"Yeah, well," Josh grinned, "somebody's gotta keep an eye on you, I guess."

"I suppose you heard what's happening to me?"

"No," Josh answered, "I didn't."

"I'm getting out. Because of my heart. I'm being mustered out."

"Oh..." Josh said simply.

"Wouldn't you like to be getting out, too?"

Josh reflected only a moment. "Yeah, I guess I would."

"I think I could arrange it."

"How—because of my head injury?"

"No. They've already given you a clean bill on that."

"Yeah—I lost my appointment to the Air Force Academy because of my hospitalization. But then they gave me a clean bill of health," Josh remarked ruefully. Then he pursued the thought. "How would you swing it—getting me discharged?"

"Well, orders came through from the Pentagon. Seems Secretary of Defense Wilson was ordered to reduce military manpower in administrative and clerical areas. The government is supposed to hire civilians for desk jobs."

JOSH

"But I've got a technical job."

"So, I'll transfer you to a desk job. We'll just help the government reduce its manpower costs. What could be more patriotic, eh?" Sgt. York grinned.

On April 1, Sgt. York, on light duty back at the base, handed Josh some official-looking military forms.

"What's this?"

"Your discharge papers."

"Uh-huh. April Fool—eh, Sarge?"

"No—I'm not kidding. They're for real. As of today, you're a civilian, McDowell."

Josh had already decided against going back home. It was too soon following his mother's death and any prolonged stay in the farmhouse brought back too many memories. He thought of his mother often, his mind wondering about the ponderings of philosophers and thinkers of the ages. He questioned the reality of some kind of afterlife. Growing up, he had been told about heaven and hell; he wondered if his Mom was in some conscious state in a mysterious afterlife dimension.

He didn't like the results of such logical thought processes. His mind more often than not rejected a concept of heaven, much as his heart wanted to claim such a belief. For this reason, and because he needed to go on with his own life, Josh went to Chicago to work. It was only a summer job. In the fall he'd enroll in college.

The men Josh worked with were not as condescending as the men in the Oliver factory were. The workers in the welding department had treated him more like a boy than a man. In many ways, he was still a boy at that time. But a year in military service had caused a great deal of growing up.

Josh's new job was to service refrigeration units for truckers hauling meats and produce. The garage was big, and the truckers could drive the big units inside to be serviced.

Once inside, though, the trucks were given more servicing than was called for on the job tickets.

CHAPTER
FOUR

Bernie showed Josh the five points of the job. A step van had been left for servicing. As soon as the driver left, Bernie drove his own car into the service area beside the van.

Josh watched as Bernie took a siphon hose from his truck and began to drain gasoline from the tank of the van into his own car.

"Fringe benefit," he grinned mischievously. "We never buy gas here. That's one of the first things you learn. See, all these trucks are company trucks. They can afford to 'contribute' to us little guys, right?"

Josh watched Bernie as he topped off his gas tank and put the siphon hose back in his truck.

"Don't worry—he ain't comin' back for four hours," Bernie reassured Josh who was looking around nervously.

"I wasn't thinking of the driver comin' back," Josh said. "I was wondering about the boss."

Bernie laughed. "Who do you think taught me how to siphon gas in the first place?" he asked.

Josh was good at the repair and servicing of refrigeration units. He also became quite experienced at siphoning gas.

There was yet another "fringe benefit" in working there. Refrigerator trucks which were fully loaded were sometimes brought in. These of course were locked to prevent pilferage. In addition to the locks—which could probably be picked—the trucks were sealed. If the seals were broken when a trucker returned, he would know someone had been stealing from his shipment.

Josh learned from Bernie and the others there was another way. Even if a trucker just stopped by for a 30-minute service call. He'd usually instruct the service mechanics to take care of his rig and went next door to the coffee shop for a half-hour or so.

In that time, Josh and Bernie would loosen the screws on the refrigeration unit mounting, attach the unit to a winch, and lift it off the truck. Once off, one of the men would slip inside the trailer through the hole for the refrigeration unit. Quickly he'd pass bounty to his buddy on top of the trailer. Hams, turkeys, boxes of steaks or fresh fruit went through the hole quickly.

Then, in minutes, the unit was serviced, put back and the screws tightened down again. The men would usually be climbing off the rig or wiping their oily hands with shop rags about the time the unsuspecting driver returned. After checking the locks and seals on the doors of the trailer, he'd sign the job ticket and be on his way—usually 50 or 100 pounds lighter than before.

Such activities began to take a toll of Josh's conscience, however. He felt *guilty*. All his life he had been conditioned by his father to put in an *honest* day's work. His mother, too, would be appalled if she knew of his dishonest dealings now. In fact, it even annoyed him that he couldn't be certain she *wasn't* aware. Sure, she had died, but what if—in some afterlife form—she was able to observe him, check up on him? It wasn't long before he was less and less a co-conspirator.

By late August, Josh drove back to Michigan to enroll in college. He had money saved from his last two factory jobs and a year of military service.

He enrolled in Kellogg College in Battle Creek. The college, like the hospital, library, and half a dozen other philanthropic institutions in the city, were there because of the famous cereal corporation. So pervasive in the community was their influence and the results of their charity, many people wondered why the town wasn't renamed for them.

Kellogg College was among the highest rated junior colleges in the state. Credits from this two-year school seemed to carry more worth when transferring—even at prestigious Big Ten universities.

Adjusting to the academic life should have been easy for Josh. After all, he graduated toward the top of his high school class. He had nearly a year of highly specialized technical training in the Air Force. And he was ready now— with that experience behind him—to settle down and take his studies seriously.

It was obvious after a few weeks that he was having trouble, however. Mrs. Hampton, his English teacher and freshman counselor, called him in for a conference.

"Josh," she began, "you did good work at your high school. Your grades were excellent. But I'm afraid the work wasn't good enough for college. I'd say that your work

CHAPTER
FOUR

here is...uh...well, Josh—here, you're a straight D student."

"Straight D?" Josh repeated. "But how can that be? I never tried hard in high school and got good grades. Here I'm really working."

"Maybe so. But I think the problem is mainly with your English."

"What do you mean?"

"Well, I suspect that your school, your high school teachers, weren't as serious about this area as they should have been," Mrs. Hampton explained. "Perhaps it served you well for your community because perfect English isn't necessarily the most important consideration."

Josh listened to her carefully. She was not putting down his town or school. Rather she recognized, "Dairy farmers and factory workers aren't always expected to work with perfect English."

"Yeah, the cows aren't gonna correct anybody," Josh grinned.

Mrs. Hampton smiled, "And that reminds me, Josh. You need to work on your pronunciation. I wrote down some words I heard you use earlier that illustrate what I mean. It's *Battle Creek,* not *Baddle Crick.* And *because,* not *becuz; when,* not *win.* It's *going,* not *goin'*—with a *g* on the end."

Josh seemed subdued. He remembered the attempts of his brother Jim to correct him. She sensed his mood and tried to sound encouraging. "It's true that you're a straight D student, Josh. Your English is poor—you use double negatives and incorrect grammar in the most basic usage. Your pronunciation is also poor. But—" she paused for emphasis. He looked up at her. "You have something that most students do not have. It is this quality which encourages me to think you will do well here at Kellogg."

Josh looked quizzical.

"Josh," she said folding her hands and leaning forward across the desk, "You have determination—a lot of drive."

"Yeah, I guess I do. I really want to better myself," he said quietly.

"Well, if you're willing to work, I'm willing to help you."

JOSH

"You will, Mrs. Hampton? Can you help me with my English? I mean, I don't have to get A's or anything. But I don't want to be a straight D student."

"Then do this. Let's work together on your grammar. You can work on your speech yourself. Get a tape recorder. Read into it—talk to it. Then play it back and listen to the way you sound. It will be a real eye-opener."

"I'll do it," Josh promised.

English, of course, was only one subject at Kellogg College. Josh learned how much it influenced his other courses, however, when he began to profit from Mrs. Hampton's tutoring.

His course of study was business and economics. As he became more and more confident, he also thought about a future career in law.

In addition to working on his grammar and speech, Josh saw the value of being able to memorize information and give back key facts by rote.

To improve his memory, Josh walked downtown and stopped by various store windows. At the hardware, drug or department stores he concentrated on what was on display in each window. Relaxing his mind, he stared at the contents for several minutes and tried to memorize. Then he walked away to see how many items he could recall. Once he had mastered this, Josh concentrated on the size, color and price of each item from memory. After practicing this for several months he could mentally project in his mind a visual image of the store window and recall every item, and describe every aspect of it correctly.

He learned he could do the same thing with information from his classes. Instead of the store window, he drew up a sheet of paper with 36 categories—with six columns across and six down. In each of these boxes he wrote pertinent facts to memorize. When it came time to recall this information for an exam, Josh simply visualized which "window" had the necessary items on display and wrote down the answers. After this, he went from being a straight D student to one getting all A's. This is not to say his grades came easy after that. It was still hard for Josh and he labored over his grammar and pronunciation. The tape recorder served as a dispassionate critic, however. After hundreds of

CHAPTER
FOUR

hours of talking for the tape recorder and listening carefully
to his speech patterns, Josh became self-conscious—in a
positive way—about how he sounded (and how he wanted to
sound.)

Between studies, Josh worked part time. Because of
his Chicago summer job, he landed a job doing refrigerator
servicing for the local A & W root beer stand. He also worked
behind the counter of the soda fountain in Dick Coward's
pharmacy. Dick was an ideal boss. He gave raises before Josh
even asked; he gave Josh time off to study for tests and
arranged for him to have flexible work hours.

Josh didn't have much time for a social life in
college. His work, studies and tutoring with Mrs. Hampton
took all his spare time.

Most of the other students were serious, too. Only a
few spent their time drinking or partying.

Josh had no time to fool around, but his thoughts
weren't always in a serious vein. For one class, he was
assigned a project—"How to get the State of Michigan out of
debt." Josh's paper, while whimsical, was backed up with
economic facts and figures to make his ideas plausible. His
plan: First, sell the Upper Peninsula to Wisconsin; second,
place all the prostitutes in the state capitol on the state
government payroll and have all the proceeds go to the
government. He used statistics to show that just 50% of the
income generated by the prostitutes could get the state out of
debt. The idea must have had feasibility because his professor
gave him an A on the paper.

His professor also encouraged Josh to seriously
consider law as a career. They discussed the possibility several
times that first year in college.

It was not merely an "I've made up my mind to do
it" decision on Josh's part. He quite carefully listed the pros
and cons of such a decision. Then he mapped out a strategy
even more ambitious than that suggested by his professor.

Not only would Josh enter the legal profession; it
would be for him a stepping stone to the goal he set for
himself. Within a 25-year plan, he reasoned, he would become
the governor of the State of Michigan.

Over a period of days stretching into weeks, his
strategy was fleshed out. When he finished, Josh had mapped

JOSH

50 six-month periods—goals, objectives and concrete plans for 25 years. The first step was to enter and win a responsible political position in college. Following that, he'd go into local politics and move up the ladder toward his goal.

His advisor looked over his plans and approved them, then encouraged him to step out and implement the strategy.

Josh ran for and was elected to the position of freshman class president, and checked off the first few objectives of the first six-month plan.

"Have you thought of a project for your term paper next year?" Mrs. Hampton asked Josh one day. "You'll be expected to work nearly all year on that project," she reminded him, "and it should have real substance."

Josh nodded. "I've been thinking about it. I have a few ideas, but haven't fully made up my mind yet."

"Why don't you take your experiences and put them together in some way? I think you already have enough to write a book."

Josh grinned, "I guess you're right. But I've already decided it should be something to help advance my master plan."

"I see," his teacher said.

"I've been thinking about something which has been on my mind for some time now. I got to thinking about it when my mother died, and became pretty well convinced of it when I visited a church in Philadelphia last winter," Josh reflected.

"Something philosophical?" Mrs. Hampton guessed.

"Yeah, sort of. I thought of it when we were doing a critique of historical events in class this semester. You know, testing the reliability of historical events based on evidence—not just believing everything you read," Josh told her.

"Then what will be your topic—something to do with English history...the Magna Carta?"

"No..." Josh replied thoughtfully. "I plan to do a serious historical study which will—once and for all—refute Christianity as nothing but meaningless fables."

CHAPTER FIVE

JOSH

JOSH WAS CHALLENGED BY HIS COLLEGE PROFESSOR'S INSISTENCE to intellectually examine every aspect of thought and truth. "Don't buy everything you're told," he told his class. "Examine these areas for yourself."

It was this premise which led Josh to set out to refute Christianity. As he thought back over his own experience with God, with religion, he had never really examined it for himself. His mother had trained him to be respectful of religious matters.

As Josh thought about it, his mother's concern could have been more from fear than anything else. He recalled going forward last year in that church in Philadelphia. It made him angry to think about it now. That something magical was supposed to take place was absurd. Nothing had happened to him—those poor people were merely fooling themselves into thinking there was something real about religion.

It was just a ritual—the tradition of going through the motions. In China, Buddhists do the same thing. In Turkey, Muslims; in Israel, Jews. All religions, he thought, are pretty much the same. A codified system of rigid thought, some ethics and patterns of worship. But for what? Could any of it be true just because someone said so?

"Take the resurrection of Jesus Christ," Josh said to a classmate in the student coffee shop one day. "That's probably the biggest myth of all. Then what about all those other miracles and things that were supposed to have happened? The proof contradicts so much of it I don't see how any intelligent person can believe it's true. Like Adam and

Eve...the flood...Jonah and the whale...and the miracles of Jesus," Josh said.

"If the world didn't evolve—if it was created by God," he added, "how do you explain those fossils in Field Museum?"

"Sh-h...not so loud," his classmate warned. "See those guys over there? Well, they're Christians. Don't talk too loudly."

"Those guys are Christians?" Josh asked.

"Yeah, why?"

"Oh, nothing. It's just...well, usually the Christians I've met are *duds*. Some of that group are in my classes. They're sharp. Are you *sure* they're Christians?"

"Yeah, well, maybe they'll help you with your project. You could ask them to help you refute Christianity," his friend joked.

"That's not such a dumb idea," Josh replied. "Most Christians pride themselves on knowing their Bibles. I'll see what they really know."

Over the next few months, Josh was both attracted to and frustrated with that small group of Christians which met regularly on campus.

He learned that the six he observed were often joined by two faculty members, also Christians, who met with them regularly.

Josh had seen the group not only in the student coffee shop, but sometimes on the campus lawn, in the library, lounges and other locations within the school.

From time to time Josh even asked them questions, and each time they responded graciously. Sometimes his questions provoked animated discussions. Other times he drew helpless stares.

Yet, one thing was overwhelmingly clear. Their lives were somehow quite different from other students on campus.

It was not a matter of superior moral standards. Josh also had those qualities. He neither drank nor smoked, nor did he participate in illicit sex. The Christians, of course, believed such things were wrong. Josh's moral code was the

CHAPTER
FIVE

same, so the difference must have been the result of something else.

Education? Determination? Josh had those qualities, too.

What is it then that sets these lives apart? Josh asked himself. One day he decided to find out. He asked Toni Lamb, the pretty green-eyed blond in the group. "I've been watching you guys," he told her. "Why are your lives so different from the other leaders on campus? What's changed your lives?" he asked.

Toni's answer was simple. It sounded too pat. "Jesus Christ," was her brief reply.

"Oh, for heaven's sake, don't give me that garbage!" Josh snapped. Then, he softened. "I'm sorry...I didn't mean to jump down your throat. It's just that, well, I believe religion *is* a bunch of garbage."

"What do you mean?" Toni asked.

"I'm fed up with church, with the Bible, with religion."

"Excuse me, but I didn't say 'religion.' You asked me why our lives are different, and I said, 'Jesus Christ.' The *person* of Jesus Christ."

Puzzled, Josh wrinkled up his nose. "What's the difference?"

"Is it true that you're working on a paper to refute Christianity?" one of the other students interrupted.

"Yes, why?" Josh asked.

"Have you ever intellectually examined the claims of Jesus Christ?"

"Intellectually examined?" Josh repeated. "I thought Christianity was a *faith*—that you parked your brain outside when you went in to church." Josh enjoyed the feeling that this sarcasm gave him. It encouraged him to make a few more jabs at their expense. They seemed to take the remarks good-naturedly, however.

"Christianity is supposed to be accepted by faith. It's a philosophical belief. But I want something that makes sense to me intellectually," Josh explained. "You Christians believe anything you're told about your faith, without ever questioning its truth or credibility."

The young man who spoke earlier stood up.

"Look," he said, "if you're going to be intellectually honest, you have to approach your search for truth without any preconceived bias. You're like the guy who says 'don't confuse me with the facts, I've already made up my mind.' Granted, a lot of Christians are like that, too. But I challenge you to honestly and intellectually examine Christianity."

Another student took his Bible and pointed to a passage he had looked up. "Here, read these verses* in First Corinthians 15. The Apostle Paul says that the resurrection is at the heart of the gospel. Prove the resurrection did not occur and Christianity will collapse."

"That's what I plan to do."

"Fine. Then I'm not concerned about the results."

Josh resented his attitude. It smacked of arrogance and he told him so.

"No, it's not arrogance," he answered. "It's just that I know what the outcome will be."

"Listen," Toni interrupted, "while you're looking into the subject, why don't you come to church with us and study from that aspect, too?"

"I will," Josh grinned, "if the girls who attend are all as pretty as you."

Toni blushed and smiled.

"Tell me how to get to your church and what time the services start," Josh said to them.

About that time Josh met another group of believers and decided to accept Toni's challenge to go to church and check it all out. But instead of going to Toni's church, he went to Factoryville Bible Church. The truth was, it was not so much to check out the church but to get to know Jeannie, one of those "Christian girls" he had just met—that's where she attended. After church, Jeannie agreed to go out with Josh. However, he noticed quite a few of their dates were at church events or services. Josh didn't mind, however, because he began to feel at home at the small church.

The pastor, Rev. Fay Logan, was a warm and friendly man in his fifties and an interesting speaker. Just by coming to services on Sunday and Wednesday night, Josh was learning much about Toni's and Jeannie's Christianity. Some

*1 Corinthians 15:12-20

*CHAPTER
FIVE*

of what he was learning was inconsistent with his precon-
ceptions.

Josh read the Bible carefully, as well as critiques
and commentaries on the Scriptures. The Christian student
was right—the weakest link for Christianity is the resurrection. He was certain there was a wealth of good material to
refute it.

However, Josh had taken the challenge to *honestly*
examine the matter, to search out the truth. Although he
mocked the Christian students for having a philosophical bias
favoring Christianity, it was a revelation of sorts for him to
discover he had an anti-supernatural philosophical bias. Truth
could not result unless he was absolutely objective.

It was one thing to dismiss something as myth or
untrue on the basis of a preconceived philosophical bias. It
was quite another matter to evaluate it honestly on the basis
of the evidence. But how?

Certainly not scientific evidence. It was impossible
to duplicate events which happened 2,000 years ago. Then
how do you examine them? Through use of *historical
evidence.*

According to the laws of legal evidence used in the
courts (as he was learning in classes) there were tests he could
apply in seeking the truth. Historical testimony can be used as
evidence if it meets the usual tests of evidence: Is the
historical testimony reliable? Do accurate written records
exist, as well as different eyewitness accounts? Do all of these
agree with the known facts?

In the process of trying to intellectually refute
Christianity, Josh was amazed to learn he had discovered 119
separate events or situations to explain away before he could
honestly and intellectually reject Jesus Christ.

Among them were the uniqueness of the Bible, of
God and Jesus. Jesus Christ had claimed to be God. Either he
was—or else He *wasn't*. If He wasn't, Josh reasoned, then He
was either a liar or lunatic. A "good man" would not make
false claims, deceive people and say He was God if it were not
true.

Another fact astounded him. According to the rules
of legal evidence, the weight of historical testimony *confirmed*

the resurrection of Christ. In fact, he discovered that the resurrection of Jesus Christ was one of the best established facts of history.

As the evidence began to mount against his position, Josh was also swayed from another direction.

At first he had gone to Factoryville Bible Church because its coeds were so attractive and because he dated Jeannie regularly. However, one day it occurred to him that he was attending even when Jeannie was out of town visiting her cousin.

The pastor was also having a subtle influence on Josh.

Finally his research and study began to have a strange effect. Josh was at war with himself. His heart told him that three things were true:

—Christ claimed to be the Son of God.
—The resurrection really happened.
—The Scriptures were reliable.

Yet, although his emotions accepted the validity of these truths, his mind and will refused to go along.

"It just can't be," he told himself. "Such things just can't happen. It's absolutely illogical."

Yet, the more he thought about it, the more convinced he was. Still, his mind would not capitulate.

One night, he went to bed at ten o'clock with these warring thoughts still racing in his brain. At four a.m. he was still awake, arguing with himself. All the next day his mind was on the matter.

After dinner that evening, Josh returned to his room to study. He had never really exercised prayer before, but now he tried.

"Jesus..." he began awkwardly, "I guess I believe in spite of myself...I believe You're real."

He recalled his former antagonism and apologized for it. As Josh thought about his actions, he was reminded of Rev. Logan's sermons and teaching. It was all coming together. His mind, will and emotions found agreement. Josh recognized he had been wrong—sinful, to use Rev. Logan's term. "Forgive me, Lord," he prayed. "The best way I know

CHAPTER
FIVE

how, I give myself to You—all of me. I want You to come into my life as You did to Toni, Jeannie, Eddie and the others. Change me and make me like them. I want what they have, and I want you to forgive me and clean up my life."

The prayer was honest, forthright. Nothing happened. He still didn't feel any different. Yet, he believed a change had taken place.

On Sunday, Josh went forward to affirm his decision publicly. Pastor Fay Logan prayed with him and defined more fully what had happened to him. He explained Josh's restlessness as God's Spirit working in his life, his apology to God for his past as repentance and the prayer of commitment as the first step in Josh's conversion. It all fit together now.

"You've been thinking Christianity was religion—a list of things to do and not do. But now, as you can see, Christianity is a relationship with Jesus," Rev. Logan explained.

"Can it really be that simple?" Josh asked.

"Get into the Bible. See what the Apostle Paul, Jesus and Peter say. Read the Gospels because you'll have a whole new understanding now. God's Spirit is within you—to instruct you."

◇——◇——◇

The January snows were piled on both sides of the path across the Kellogg campus. Josh heard his name and turned to see who called.

"Russ," he smiled, "how are you? I haven't seen you in a while."

"I'm fine, Josh," he waved. "Hey, I heard the news. About you becoming a Christian, I mean."

"Yeah, about six weeks ago."

"Well, I just wanted to tell you I'm a Christian too."

"Really? That's great."

"—and I'm really excited for you. I think it's beautiful what God is doing in your life!"

"You *do?*"

"Well, yes—of course," Russ replied, caught off guard by Josh's question.

JOSH

"Russ," Josh said quietly, "why didn't *you* tell me about Jesus? If you knew the Christian life was so great, why did you wait? Why didn't you share it with me?"

"Uh...yeah, well," Russ stammered, "I...I guess I should have...."

Josh watched as Russ walked away, obviously uncomfortable. He had not intended to embarrass him. The question was not asked with belligerence. Josh simply wondered why a Christian would keep such good news a secret.

It was true—God *was* working in Josh's life. While the results were not as obvious to others, there was one way Josh knew a supernatural event had occurred.

His hatred for his father had miraculously melted. He had confessed to God his feelings for his dad and prayed that he could forgive him and be himself forgiven by God in the process.

It happened as quickly as his asking.

No longer was his father a drunken creature to be hated and abused. Josh saw instead a man who helped give him life, a man with flawed character, to be sure. But "all have sinned," the Bible reminded him. This was not to excuse everything of the past; rather it was to understand it.

There was excitement and exhilaration in Josh's voice when he called his father to tell him two things he'd never told him before.

"Dad, I've become a Christian...and...Dad—I love you."

CHAPTER SIX

"BY GOD'S GRACE, I'VE BEEN ABLE TO DEVELOP one of the most successful law practices in the state of Michigan," the man was saying, "but I want everyone here to know that Jesus Christ is more important to me than my law practice."

Josh listened as the well-dressed lawyer spoke to the congregation of the Factoryville Bible Church. It impressed him that an attorney would give a testimony for Jesus Christ in a church. He wondered if he would get up in front of people like that—poised, self-assured, confident—and speak about Christ.

Following the service, Josh worked his way toward the front of the church and introduced himself to the lawyer.

"I plan to enter the legal profession, too," Josh told him. "I think I can really be effective as a Christian there."

The lawyer looked at Josh for a long moment, then said, "No...don't go into law. If you want to serve Christ, think about another career."

Josh was puzzled and wanted to pursue the matter, but others were shaking hands with the speaker and their conversation cut off. He shrugged off the comment and drove back to the college.

◇ ◇ ◇

Josh and Jeannie were steady dates throughout his second year of college. There was no doubt in her mind that they would get married after college—probably before Josh enrolled in Law School.

JOSH

Josh was still following his strategy for a career in law and politics. His new-found Christian faith only sharpened his desires and fueled his ambition.

He had been promised a complete law library worth $35,000 upon completion of law school, and his academic work reflected his seriousness.

As the weather grew warmer, Josh often drove out to a gravel pit at the edge of town. The bulldozers and earth-moving equipment had carved out a rough amphitheater from the hill. It was here—to a few cynical crows and nervous ground squirrels—that Josh began to "preach." His speech and public speaking classes had given him the basic skills and his visits to Rev. Logan's church provided him with the example. Now, with material gleaned from his studies, he preached sermons in the otherwise empty gravel pit.

After awhile, Josh wanted to try out his talks on a "live" audience. He drove to Lansing or Detroit on Saturdays, parking his car near a skid row mission. He had called earlier in the week asking, "Would it be all right if I came and gave my testimony?"

Occasionally, he gave his testimony in church. Soon he was asked to speak to the high school youth group or a Sunday school class.

At one such occasion, a woman sat in the church caught up in his excitement and message. She was a secretary for the Rev. Carl McIntire and mentioned to her employer that he ought to look up this young man from Kellogg College.

Josh spent the summer of 1960 in Europe as a part of a youth outreach sponsored by Rev. Carl McIntire.

He had scraped together the necessary funds for his travel expenses and went as the speaker for the group of young people.

The summer was a fantastic experience for Josh. He spoke in churches and in prayer groups in Great Britain and studied in Beatenberg, Switzerland. During free time, he visited British courts and talked to English barristers about their trial law. He was even an invited guest of some 50 top

*CHAPTER
SIX*

legal minds in Britain who shared experiences with him and showed off their vast legal libraries.

His interest in law was as strong as ever following that tour. However, he was also beginning to realize that perhaps God was calling him to be involved full time in a teaching or speaking ministry. How the two could be reconciled was not clear to him.

Rev. Fay Logan was always available for counsel. As Josh talked to him about his dual interests in law and a speaking ministry, Rev. Logan thought for a few moments. Then he said, "You know, I think you ought to go to Wheaton College next year instead of the university."

"Wheaton? Where's that—Maryland?"

"Illinois. It's where Billy Graham went to school."

"Billy Graham? Really? Tell me about it."

"Well," Rev. Logan explained, "I think it's the one school to help you settle your dilemma. If you plan to go into law, they'll prepare you to be the *best* Christian lawyer." The minister looked out the window of his study, then turning to Josh, leaned across his desk to confide, "Our church doesn't approve of Wheaton College. But I don't think you have to be concerned. With your hunger for intellectual knowledge to go with spiritual truth, I think this is the school for you. Yessir, the more I think about it, Wheaton is for you."

Rev. Logan reached for the telephone and called the registrar of the school. However, because the school was trying to establish a policy of accepting only those who would attend all four years, and since Josh had already attended Kellogg College for two years, they discouraged the transfer.

Rev. Logan was persistent. He knew how to pull a few strings, and Josh was officially enrolled for the fall term.

Adjusting to academic life at Wheaton was terribly difficult for Josh—as hard as the adjustment to Kellogg from his rural high school. He hardly dated—not because his relationship with Jeannie was so serious—they had agreed to date others while he was away. Rather, he did not date because there was simply no time to do so. Studies occupied nearly every free hour during the week. Josh was busy on Saturdays and holidays at the lucrative painting contracting business he started. On Sundays he was often away on some speaking engagement.

Summers he stayed in Wheaton for an extra heavy load of classes in summer school. This was also the best time of year for the painting business. During summers, especially, Josh earned as much as $1,000 a week painting houses, which allowed him to pay for his education.

Letters from Jeannie were frequent and becoming more and more serious. She often wrote of her plans and dreams for after their marriage. Even though they had talked about it Josh had never really proposed marriage to her—but she interpreted his silence as agreement.

His letters to her were few, and when he did write, he told of his school interests and accomplishments. He told her about Dr. Robert Culver, who taught his Bible class. The Bible was unfamiliar to Josh as a new believer. No doubt the questions he asked Dr. Culver were elementary, but Dr. Culver was always patient when Josh asked him to define terms such as sanctification or justification.

Dr. Samuel Schultz taught Old Testament Survey and encouraged Josh to learn about and thoroughly appreciate the Scriptures. Yet, at the same time, it was Dr. Schultz who encouraged Josh to pursue a career in law. "You have great aptitude for law, Josh," he told the young student. "You'll be a great lawyer—with your mind you should go into law."

All his professors demanded the best from him. His academic work did not come easy. It wasn't so much a matter of memorizing facts as he had done at Kellogg. Now he was being asked to think, to discover truth, and apply it in his search for knowledge.

Josh responded to their encouragement and demands for excellence. "I never in my life wanted to be mediocre," he told Dr. William Volkman, another professor, one day. "I've never had to be 'number one'," he said, "but I always want to do my best."

He recalled having discussed the matter with Rev. Logan before he left for Wheaton. "What makes the dif-

ference in people?'' he asked his pastor. ''Some people are on
fire for the Lord. Others have lives not worth living. What is
it that makes the difference?''

"Tell you what," his pastor had told him then,
"when you get to Wheaton, you find the most dynamic and
spiritual students you can find and get to know them. Study
with them. Room with them. Follow them. Get to *really* know
them. Then I think you'll find out for yourself."

Now, at Wheaton, Josh looked around for those
qualities in the lives of students. He found Frank Keifer, a
senior, who always seemed to be having a prayer meeting in
his room. Jim Green was the kind of student who never
compromised his convictions. Dick Purnell, a junior like Josh,
was always deep in the study of God's Word and actively
shared his faith. These men are still some of Josh's closest
friends.

Josh lived in a rooming house with three rooms for
students. His roommate was, to phrase it mildly, a real
character. He plastered pictures all over the walls of nature
scenes, then burned incense and meditated, staring at the
pictures for hours. He never washed his clothes. Josh recoiled
each time he opened the closet door. Instead of laundering his
dirty clothes and underwear, the student merely bought new
clothes. Josh began to look for a different roommate.

At this time, Dick Purnell roomed across the hall
with two other men. One Saturday morning, Bill, one of the
two, ran into Josh's room to solicit his help with a prank.

"Dick's bringing Ruth to his room," Bill said.
"Come on, let's play a trick on them."

The floor was "off limits" to women students, of
course. However, since he thought his roommates were gone,
Dick Purnell thought there would be no harm in his girl
friend's visit—particularly if he maintained discretion and
kept the door to his room open.

Josh and Bill, meanwhile, waited until the couple
was inside and comfortably engaged in small talk. Then they
quietly took the big galvanized mop bucket from the utility
room downstairs and filled it with water in the basement. The
two conspirators then quietly tip-toed upstairs and sneaked
into the bathroom, across the hall from Dick's room.

Leaving the door ajar—as would be the case in a

typical "men only" dorm, Bill began whistling loudly while Josh carried the big bucket over to the toilet.

Dick and Ruth heard the whistling and saw, with growing embarrassment, that the bathroom door was ajar. Crimson-faced, Ruth stood, nearly panic-stricken—unsure whether to stay or leave. She *couldn't* leave, because if she did, she'd walk straight into—

The whistling gave way to a loud and unmistakable sound of water (being slowly poured from the bucket into the toilet) which neither she nor Dick could see. They of course suspected the noise to be what it sounded like and sat in mutual embarrassment. The trickling water continued for over five minutes as the four-gallon mop bucket was slowly emptied. It was the longest period in history. Josh and Bill couldn't contain their laughter any longer. Their guffaws lightened the moment somewhat when the couple learned what had taken place. But it did have its effect. Dick Purnell never again asked a woman student to his room.

Such good-natured moments helped balance the tensions of study and work for Josh.

Josh enjoyed Wheaton, Illinois, the community in Chicago's western suburbs where his college was located. The seasons were like those of his native Michigan, and the town was far enough from Chicago to hold some of the same rural Michigan charms.

It seemed as if everywhere he drove in the small community, people were friendly and the homes were quiet and picturesque. Josh didn't even mind having to stop periodically for a train crossing gate. The town seemed to have them everywhere, but usually when they came down, the clanging bells and flashing lights meant a commuter train was crossing. And these generally went by quickly.

One day, as one of the gates lowered, he pulled his car to a stop. He glanced down the track and saw it was another commuter. It would be here momentarily and he'd be on his way. No need to be impatient at railroad crossings in this town.

Casually Josh glanced in his rear view mirror. His

CHAPTER
SIX

gaze froze and he instinctively braced his body. A car was
coming toward him with obviously no intention of stopping.

A drunken driver had not seen the train crossing
gate or Josh's stopped auto. His car hit Josh's at 45 m.p.h.,
causing a collision which nearly pushed Josh's auto into the
path of the on-coming commuter train.

There seemed to be no physical damage to Josh
personally. However, the next day he was in severe pain. An
examining physician said, "You're fortunate, son. It's bad,
but could have been worse. Almost caused you a broken neck.
If that had happened, you'd have been paralyzed...if you'd
have lived."

Recovery was slow. Josh was placed in a cast and
traction.

While he recovered in the college infirmary, Dick
Purnell and other friends dropped by to cheer him up and
pray with him. They brought him up to date on the latest
pranks or incredible assignments the professors had given.

Dr. V. Raymond Edman also came by to visit. He
was president of Wheaton College and Josh was impressed
that he would come by to spend 2½ hours with one of the
students. Yet, he seemed more like a consoling, friendly
pastor than a college administrator when he prayed with Josh.

On another day, Josh had a visit from Rev. Torrey
Johnson, who had heard about his injury. Josh was even
more surprised at his visit than he was at Dr. Edman's. Rev.
Johnson, then pastor of the First Evangelical Free Church of
Wheaton, was one of the founders, with Billy Graham, of
Youth for Christ. He was also a famous speaker.

Josh told Torrey Johnson of his own dreams of
becoming a speaker.

Rev. Johnson said, "I'd like to help you, son. I'll
write you some letters of introduction. I know a lot of people
in this country who could use a good youth speaker—
especially a lot of YFC clubs. I'll send out a letter endorsing
you so they'll know they ought to use you."

"Man, that's really generous, sir," Josh said. "I
appreciate that. Coming from you, that's quite an honor."

When he was able to travel, the college thought he

might recover better if he were at home in his own bed. He still wore a neck brace and suffered excruciating pain and crippling headaches. His arms and neck were in traction.

Josh's dad welcomed his son, although Josh knew his father had been drunk the night of the accident. Confusion had resulted at the hospital when they had tried to notify his family.

Dad was sober now, though. In fact, he was sober more and more these days. Since Josh had called to tell him about becoming a Christian, the old man had thought seriously about getting his own life together. He had been going to meetings of *Alcoholics Anonymous.* That seemed to help some, but he had not yet given up drinking altogether.

For several days, Josh's dad carefully looked after his son. The senior McDowell had struggled since his wife's death to develop basic skills with meals and housework.

"Thanks, Dad," Josh said as he put the empty tray on the end of his bed. "Thanks for taking care of me."

The father shrugged. "It's nothing. How are you doing?"

"Okay...except for the headaches. They're murder," Josh said.

For a long moment the man gazed at his son. His sun-wrinkled face seemed softer now, as if time had erased some of the hardness and sharp edges. The old man's eyes began to water, giving way to tears.

It was the first time Josh had ever seen his father cry. "Y-you're different now, Josh," he cried. "You've changed. You don't act like you hate me anymore."

"I don't, Dad," Josh replied softly. "I love you."

"Do you mean it?"

"Yes, Dad. I mean it. I love you."

"B-but how...how can you love somebody like—" his father stammered.

"Last year I couldn't, Dad," Josh explained, and tenderly shared with his father how Jesus Christ had taken all the hate out of his life and had given him a brand new capacity to love. "I asked Jesus to forgive me and personally take over my life," he added.

"Son..." the father groped for the words. "Son, if God will work in my life that way—the way He's worked in

CHAPTER
SIX

yours—to let you love someone the likes of me, then I think
He can handle my drinking problem. Will you help me?''

Josh's own eyes now filled with tears as he reached
out against the restraining braces to touch his father's hand.

In the next moments he explained to his father how
to ask God for forgiveness and pray to receive Christ into his
life. Josh's dad's conversion to Christianity was genuine, a
glorious, dramatic separation from the past. God—as Josh
promised—made him a ''new creation'' in Christ.

A lifetime of craving for alcohol was gone. There
was no way to explain it except as a miracle; that's exactly
what his dad began to do. He cornered everyone in town and
excitedly shared what Jesus had done in his life—and just as
enthusiastically tried to get them to make the same decision he
had made.

After his recovery from the auto accident injury,
Josh went back to Wheaton College to resume his studies.

His father, meanwhile, had his entire life transformed and everyone in Union City learned about it.

After becoming a Christian, Josh's dad began to
travel to other places in Michigan to share his testimony of
how God had delivered him from alcoholism. The talk was
especially effective in missions and prisons as men whose lives
had been nearly destroyed by alcohol abuse responded to what
had happened in his life.

However, as wonderful and effective as his talks
were, they could not match the sense of satisfaction Josh's
father found in the new relationship with his son.

Neither Josh nor his dad could believe their
closeness now—and both regretted the wasted years when they
were estranged. Yet, the Lord seemed to be redeeming the
situation by giving them such an affinity for one another now.

CHAPTER SEVEN

FOR THEIR SENIOR YEAR AT WHEATON COLLEGE, Josh and Dick Purnell decided to move to a different rooming house and become roommates. Josh recalled Rev. Logan's advice to find the most spiritual and motivated students and let their influences rub off on him.

This new arrangement made studying easier too, since there were no other students in the house to distract from the seriousness of their work.

In addition to their daily studies and homework, both Dick and Josh had weekend projects which involved them in a regular ministry. Ironically these were the two areas which made each angry and jealous of the other.

Dick visited colleges and universities which were within driving distance of Wheaton. Often he came back from the University of Illinois, University of Wisconsin, Northern Illinois University or other schools after an evangelistic excursion with Pete Gillquist or other staff members of a new organization called *Campus Crusade for Christ.*

Josh listened as Dick explained how he had shared the gospel with some students at these schools and related how one or two would pray to receive Jesus Christ after each visit.

Dick, meanwhile, would hear Josh talk about his speaking engagements in various places over the weekends of the school year.

Josh wanted for himself the experience Dick told about of leading someone to Christ. And Dick wished he could travel around the country and speak to different groups as Josh did.

But neither spoke to the other about this frustration and irritation. Instead, they just put aside their real feelings.

Josh was introduced to the dynamic man behind the Campus Crusade movement when Bill Bright came to Wheaton College that fall. Bright was a brilliant and highly motivating force whose own life had been transformed by the gospel. A former successful businessman, Bright gave it all up to start an evangelistic outreach to secular university students.

His method was to recruit, train and disciple Christian leadership from evangelical colleges and universities. Once trained, they were sent to various universities to start Campus Crusade works on those campuses.

On one of these recruiting visits to Wheaton College, Bill Bright had challenged the student·body in a chapel service. Following that, Josh—along with Dick Purnell and Jim Green—met with him in the student coffee shop.

Time was suspended as Josh and the others sat in rapt attention to Bright. "Men, you already know the power of Christ to transform lives. You've·seen Him at work in your own life when He saved you," Bright said to them. "But let me share a concept with you that will add a whole new dimension to your life."

Bright took a napkin and began to draw some diagrams. "There are three kinds of people in the world. The Bible tells us there is the 'natural man,' the 'spiritual man' and the 'carnal man.' The natural man is one who hasn't received the Lord Jesus as Saviour. The carnal man is one who has received Christ, but lives a defeated life because he trusts in his own efforts to live the Christian life."

"What do you mean, sir?" Josh asked.

Bright drew a circle on the napkin and a crude chair inside. "Let's say this is the life of a carnal man—a Christian, but one whose life is self-controlled. Ego—or self—is on the throne in that man's life. Christ is made to stand aside while this man pursues his own interests.

"But the spiritual man," explained Bright, drawing another diagram, "places Christ on the throne of his life and his own ego steps aside to allow God's Holy Spirit to control his life."

Bright looked into the eager faces of the students. "The spiritual man demonstrates unique personal traits in his

CHAPTER
SEVEN

life," he continued. "The 'fruits of the Spirit'—love, joy, peace, patience, kindness, faithfulness and goodness—are obvious benefits. These characteristics are reflected in greater or lesser degree—depending on the maturity of the Christian who places Christ on the throne in his life—and the consistency of his doing so."

SELF-CONTROLLED LIFE   **CHRIST-CONTROLLED CHRISTIAN**   **THE CARNAL CHRISTIAN**

"Men," Bright smiled, "how would you like to appropriate the fullness and power of the Holy Spirit?"

Josh, Dick and Jim all agreed that their lives should be controlled by God's Holy Spirit, which Bright explained was an act of faith—as is the means by which we receive the forgiveness of salvation.

"Father..." Josh prayed in the coffee shop booth, "I need You. I can see that I have been in control of my own life—trying to live the Christian life without Your help. No wonder I have sinned so often since becoming a Christian. Lord, I thank You that I was able to invite Jesus into my life to forgive me for my sins. Now, I ask the Holy Spirit to take control—reign on the throne of my life. Fill me with Your love and Your power. And Lord, help me demonstrate the qualities of the Spirit-filled life in my character."

The others prayed similar prayers before Bill Bright left.

Dr. V. Raymond Edman, president of Wheaton College, had seen revival break out on campus before. It was his prayer that it would happen to every class going through the college.

JOSH

To this end, he had asked his friend, Dr. Richard Halverson, pastor of Fourth Presbyterian Church in Washington, D.C., to be speaker for the annual "Spiritual Emphasis Week."

Dr. Halverson was a Wheaton alumnus and the perfect choice for the assignment. He was a brilliant Bible expositor as well as dynamic speaker.

Yet, when he spoke to the combined student body in the new Edman Chapel on Monday morning and evening, he felt uncomfortable. The students seemed cold, unresponsive—almost defiant. He couldn't define the difficulty exactly, but a wall of some kind existed between students and speaker.

The next day the situation was the same. Dr. Halverson was met not only with indifference as he spoke, but he sensed even in the hallways or in the coffee shop students were cold and—could such a thing be?—*hostile.*

By the middle of the week Dr. Halverson felt drained. He had poured everything into his messages—but they were being met with stronger and stronger resentment and coolness. He felt like calling the airport to check on the next flight back to Washington, when a delegation led by a senior student, John Huffman, approached him.

"Dr. Halverson," Huffman said, "the students...uh...don't like your messages. But it's not entirely your fault, sir."

"Oh?" Dr. Halverson asked. "What's going on? Why is there this terrible resistance?"

"I think the students know that Dr. Edman wants revival on campus. Some of them think he wants it so badly that these meetings are structured in such a way as to manipulate that. You know, sir—the stirring message, the emotion of the music, the invitation—it all seems contrived to them," explained Huffman.

"But it isn't," Dr. Halverson protested. "The last thing in the world I'd ever try to do is the work of the Holy Spirit."

"Yes, sir—I'm sure of that, too. I don't know what to tell you, Dr. Halverson," said the student leader, "but I felt you should know that the attitude of the students isn't really your fault."

*CHAPTER
SEVEN*

As the delegation left, Richard Halverson thought about what they had said. He could see how the students could get an impression of being pressured to make certain decisions. The organist, in an effort to be relevant to his message, was ever quick to respond with a hymn of deep emotion or conviction. Likewise, the song leader wrung every drop of emotion from his selection following the service.

As a result, the invitation was given in the same spirit of emotional fervor.

That, of course, is what the students resented. They assumed the invitation was a "set-up"—that somehow the speaker conspired with the musicians to manipulate the emotions of the crowd toward a desired goal.

That night, Dr. Halverson completely changed the format of the meeting.

"I've learned today that you really can't stand me," he told the students. "To be honest with you, I haven't enjoyed your company this week, either. Now, as I understand it, many of you are bothered by the way we've been giving the invitation this week. Well, all right, tell you what I'll do. I'll give you the invitation first—right now—and get it out of the way. I don't want you to get hung up on the invitation and not hear the message. So, here's what I plan to say. Actually, I'm going to read from Isaiah 6:8. It says, 'And I heard the voice of the Lord, saying, Whom shall I send, and who will go for us?' "

The students, caught off guard at his candor and spiritual honesty, listened.

"God didn't say, 'I'm going to send you—so you'd better get ready to go.' He doesn't manipulate us into agreeing to do something against our wills. All He does is say, 'Whom shall I send...who will go?' "

He paused, then said quietly, "That's going to be my invitation tonight—who will go?"

Halverson apologized for not being able to "connect" with the students, then went into a brief message. The talk was bare of emotion. He was explicit, intellectual and addressed each student's will and mind. He explained the need for specific commitment to the purposes of God and the ongoing work of His kingdom, "whether you are a doctor, lawyer or teacher," he said.

JOSH

"Remember when I explained the invitation earlier," he told them. "I won't ask you to come forward and say you'll do anything or go anywhere for God. No...all I'm asking you to do is say you're *willing* to be used. Isaiah responded by saying, 'Lord, here am I...send me.' I'm not even going to ask you to do that. Just say, 'Lord, here am I...use me. Use my talents and tools.' If you plan to be a doctor—bring your stethescope and place it on the altar. If you're an engineer, bring Him your slide rule. Tell Him it's His. Maybe He'll pick it up and say—'I want you to be an engineer.' Or maybe he'll say, 'Leave your slide rule—I have something else for you.' If you're going to be a lawyer—place your law books on the altar and say, 'Lord, here am I...use me, send me.'"

Josh McDowell looked up with a quick glance at the speaker. It was as if he had addressed that last statement directly at him.

No. I don't want to.

"You already know the nature of the invitation," Halverson continued. "Whoever you are, whatever you plan to be, will you put your plans on the altar and be willing to be used of God? If you will, I invite you to stand—no hymn, no music—simply stand and silently make your commitment to God."

The chapel silence was broken as nearly the entire student body stood in quiet commitment.

Josh sat in his seat, however, flushed with resentment and anger. His hands were perspiring and his body suddenly uncomfortable in his seat. He knew God was asking if he was willing to be sent out in His service, but Josh did not want to respond.

He bolted out of his seat, but instead of commitment, rose in anger. Josh all but ran toward the exit doors. He pushed the panic bar so hard that it echoed throughout the entire auditorium, but he didn't care.

I don't want to go, he reminded himself.

Josh ran down the steps of Edman Chapel to the street and didn't stop running until he got to his rooming house. He stormed around his room for a while, and then he went to bed.

When Dick Purnell came in later, Josh pulled the

CHAPTER
SEVEN

covers over his head and turned away. Dick said nothing. He took out his books and started to study.

Josh got up and dressed about eleven that night and went out. He walked back and forth around the school. His mind would not rest as he walked, and he found himself downtown by the commuter train station.

He walked to 'Round the Clock, an all-night restaurant, and ordered coffee. By one a.m., he was still restlessly walking the streets. He went to Chaplain Welsh's living quarters and got him out of bed for counsel. The chaplain listened to Josh explain what had happened earlier and rubbed the sleep from his eyes. "I'm afraid I can't help you, Josh," he said. "It's your decision."

Josh went back outside and resumed his restless walking. At four a.m., he paused under a street lamp on South Union Street. It was October and the leaves had turned color and begun to fall. A dampness hung in the air yet dry leaves rustled underfoot.

He recalled his earlier conversation with Bill Bright about the Spirit-controlled life. He saw his present attitude at odds with that principle. He recognized two things: God was assuredly calling him; and, he did not want to respond.

"Lord," Josh prayed in desperation, "You know that I haven't wanted to yield to Your will. Yet, I know that I should. You must know that I'm afraid—afraid You're calling me into Christian work—and my heart is set on law. Lord, I don't want to give up law. Is that what *You* want? Can you help me to *want* to do Your will?" He paused and reflected at that thought, then resignedly prayed, "God...I can't get away from that verse—'here am I, send me.' Lord—*I'm going!* You send me...I'll go."

The final decision was not consciously made in the early hours of that October morning. Josh still kept to his agenda, and his own plans for the future. Four attorneys had already promised they'd pay Josh's law school tuition and expenses after graduation from Wheaton.

Despite this reservation, Josh seemed to be saying to God, "I'll let You have this other part of my life." He gave

JOSH

his weekends to share Christ through speaking engagements. This seemed glamorous to Dick Purnell, but—as before—Josh was jealous for Dick's ability to lead people to Christ personally.

Bill Bright had given Dick something called the Four Spiritual Laws* to which Dick had often referred in telling about his successes.

One weekend, Josh listened to an excited Dick Purnell tell of yet another adventure in leading someone to Christ.

When Dick went out, Josh began to look through his books, papers and notebooks until he found a sheet of paper with the "four laws" diagrammed.

He copied them, memorized them, then was anxious to try using them with someone. Dick and the others went to universities to explain the four laws to people, but Josh wasn't sure enough of himself to try that. Instead, he decided to take the Northwestern train to downtown Chicago. Just a few blocks from the train station was West Madison Street—Chicago's skid row.

Josh stopped four different derelicts or passersby and shared the four laws with them, using the diagrams and Bible verses that he had copied from Dick's notebook. He was amazed that three of the four wanted to pray to receive Jesus Christ as their Savior.

This was the excitement he had been looking for. In all his speaking engagements over the past three years of his Christian experience, he had never once personally led someone to Christ, with the exception of his father. This excitement generated a deep respect for Bill Bright and the fledgling *Campus Crusade for Christ* organization.

The experience in Chicago's skid row would be repeated by Josh nearly every weekend from now on. He would preach on street corners and talk with passersby and introduce them to Jesus Christ.

"I have a philosophy** that's different from most

---

*The Four Spiritual Laws will be found on p. 213

**This philosophy of evangelism was motivated by an anonymous poem which a missionary read during a chapel service. The poem was entitled:

*CHAPTER
SEVEN*

people's,'' Josh told Dick Purnell later. "Most people pray
that the Holy Spirit will lead them to some one to whom they
can witness. I'm going to share Christ with everyone and pray
that if the Holy Spirit *doesn't* want me to speak to someone,
He'll lead me not to. Otherwise I'll talk to 'em all about
Jesus!''

Josh became so excited at the results of his witnessing that he felt compelled to talk to everyone about it.

"My Chum"
"He stood at the crossroad all alone
    with the sunrise in his face
He had no fear for the path unknown
    He was set for a manly race.
But the road stretched east and the road
stretched west
    And he didn't know which road was the best
My chum turned wrong; went down, down,
down
    'Til He lost the race and the victor's crown.
    At last he came to an ugly snare
    Because no one had stood at the crossroad
there.
Another chum on another day at the self-same
        crossroad paused
    To choose a way which would lead to the
greater
        good.
And the road stretched east and the road
stretched west
    But I was there to show him the best.
So my chum turned right and went on and on
    'Til he won the race and the victor's crown.
At last he came to the mansion fair
    Because I had stood at the crossroad there.
Since then I've raised a daily prayer
    That I be kept faithfully standing there
    To direct the runners as they come
    To save my own—or another's—chum.''

JOSH

Many people (other Christians and fellow students) who had not had that experience misunderstood his exuberance. They labeled his telling of his witnessing forays as boastful arrogance. A few people pointed out to him that he seemed to be having a problem with pride.

Josh ignored their remarks, however. Usually he just shrugged them off.

Josh heard from his dad and Jeannie. His dad called to tell about his new bride, a widow named Berta. The phone call brought up bittersweet emotions. Josh was happy and pleased that his father was enjoying life as a new Christian and they were as close now as any father and son could be.

Yet, he was sad to think that Mom was not alive to enjoy these blessings. Somehow it seemed unfair that Berta would realize the happiness of life with his father, and that his mother never saw this grace and beauty emerge from her husband's life.

The call from Jeannie came after her letter.

"You didn't answer it," she said, "and I was afraid something was wrong."

"Uh...I...I was awfully busy," Josh replied.

"I know," she answered. "But I miss you so much. I can't wait to see you again. Do you remember all the fun we've had together."

"Yes...."

"Josh," her voice was more serious now. "I've dated once or twice while you were away. I had a terrible time. It only proved how much I love you. Do you—well, you know—do you miss me?"

"Yes...I miss you a lot."

"Do you still love me?"

"I...uh..." he stammered.

"It's all right," Jeannie interrupted. "I just want you to know that I love you."

Josh admired, respected her. He had a great deal of affection for her. He was physically attracted to her. *But do I love her?* he asked himself. *What is love? Jeannie's pretty,*

CHAPTER
SEVEN

*she's smart—spiritual—has lots of super qualities. I wonder—
do I love her?*

The pressure by his friends and family was strong.
Dad thought Jeannie was absolutely the best woman in the
world for Josh. So did nearly everyone in their church and
community.

It seemed as if everyone was pressuring Josh about
Jeannie. At last he could think of no particular reason why he
shouldn't ask her to marry him.

Engagements were a special tradition for Wheaton
College seniors. When a student became engaged, his friends
had a party for the couple in "The Tower," the upper loft in
Blanchard Hall where the clock tower was located. There was
a special ceremony involved in the giving of the engagement
ring as the friends shower the lovers with good wishes and
ring the bells in the campus tower.

When Josh gave Jeannie her diamond, she was
radiant and ecstatic. He should have been happy, but was
inwardly miserable.

Later, she noticed his subdued spirit. "What's the
matter, darling?" she asked.

He didn't answer right away. When he did, he tried
to temper his response with tenderness as well as honesty.
"I'm not all that certain that I'm in love with you," Josh
admitted.

"That's all right, darling," she said, kissing his
cheek. "You'll be sure. It'll come in time. Don't worry."

Deep in his heart, though, Josh knew he should end
the relationship now. But he was afraid of hurting her.

One day Josh and Dick Purnell were driving along
before the end of school, and they began to talk about their
women friends.

"I tell you, Josh," Dick complained, "Ruth is
driving me crazy. She's fickle. One day she loves me, the next
day she doesn't know I'm alive. She couldn't care less for
me."

Josh listened, then confessed his own dilemma with
Jeannie. "Maybe I'm the fickle one in our relationship," he
admitted. "But I can't help it. Everyone expects me to marry
her. And I suppose it is the logical thing to do. But I don't

know if I love her.''

"Women," muttered Dick. "I can't believe the problems they cause us.'' He drove along quietly for several more moments, then asked his friend, "Josh, do you think God is interested in our love life?''

"Maybe we should find out. Why don't we pray and see.''

———◇——◇——◇———

A few weeks later, it was time for graduation. Dick and Josh postponed their "good-byes" to each other as long as possible. Both knew it would be a very hard emotional time and wanted to delay the feelings as long as possible.

"It's kinda sad," reflected Dick. "We've become such good friends and we'll probably never see each other again.''

"Probably not," Josh agreed. "We can stay in touch. Write me from medical school in Houston...and I'll write you from law school.''

There were brotherly embraces and wistful hand-shakes before the two separated.

The campus was active with other students, some with their parents, in the final stages of departure for the school year.

Josh had packed all his belongings into his car and sat behind the wheel before leaving. Yet, for some reason, he couldn't go. The idea of driving back to Michigan frightened him. He knew he could not go ahead with the marriage plans. He also knew he lacked the courage to break up with Jeannie.

What he needed was a trip somewhere else—a delay, a diversion—an opportunity to think of a way to break off his engagement and forget Jeannie.

He had enough money saved from his painting business so he didn't *have* to drive back to Michigan right away. Impulsively, he decided to go to California.

CHAPTER EIGHT

BEFORE HE LEFT FOR CALIFORNIA, JOSH CALLED JEANNIE. "I'm sorry," he told her, "but I'm not in love with you. It would be a mistake. I simply can't marry you."

She did not react in the way he'd expected. She responded sweetly, seeming to understand. But he could tell from her words and attitude that she was just patiently waiting for him to come to his senses.

Josh and Dave, a friend he had met through Jeannie, headed for the West Coast. They took their time and stopped to enjoy themselves as they came to various tourist attractions.

At the Grand Canyon in Arizona they even rented pack mules and took the excursion into the canyons.

This was the first time in several years that Josh's life had been so aimless. When he got to California he still had no idea why he was there. The weeks went by and an entire summer was soon gone.

Josh began to like California. Its climate and fast-paced life-style were such a contrast to his rural Michigan home that they energized him.

"I've been thinking," he told his father by telephone one day, "maybe I'll look into U.C.L.A. law school."

"But what about Michigan?" his father asked.

"I could transfer later," Josh observed.

"And what about Jeannie?" is what his father really meant to ask.

"Dad, I told her I didn't love her. It would be a mistake to get married."

"Oh..." he heard his father say. Josh could almost

weigh the disappointment in his dad's voice.

"U.C.L.A. has one of the best law schools in the country." Josh tried to change the subject. "I've already started my enrollment proceedings."

"I see," his dad said. "Well, if that's what you think is best, son. Just so you're happy."

"Oh, I am, Dad. I'm really happy," Josh said brightly. Yet, in his heart he was miserable and didn't know why.

When he hung up the phone his mind went back to Wheaton College and the week of special meetings with Richard Halverson. The speaker had asked for commitment from students who would say, "Lord, I'm willing to go into Christian service, if that's the direction You lead."

Josh, however, had already found that in his witnessing trips, God was sending people his way who needed to hear about Christ. He knew if he were to say, "Lord, I'm willing," the matter would end. The need was so obvious, what additional convincing would be required?

"Lord," Josh prayed, "You know I could never be a full-time Christian worker. My skills are in training to be a lawyer. I'm not a good speaker. My grammar is bad—I stammer. I don't see any potential at all."

The conviction would not leave him however.

"All right, Lord," he continued, "I'll go into Christian work unless You shut the door."

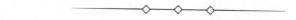

A week later, Josh was browsing through a Christian magazine and came across an ad for a California-based theological seminary.

"I'll make plans to enroll in seminary," he thought. "If they accept me today, then I'll know it's God's will. If God closes that door, then I'll go ahead with my plans to go to U.C.L.A."

Josh drove to La Mirada, south of Los Angeles, and located Talbot Theological Seminary, on the campus of Biola College. It was Friday afternoon and classes for the fall term were to start Monday.

He went to the registrar's office to apply for admission.

CHAPTER
EIGHT

"But classes start on Monday, sir," the woman at the desk told him. "Do you have an application turned in?"

"No—I just learned about your school this week," Josh told her.

"I see. Well, I'm afraid we're not going to be able to help you. You see, the process is like this—you turn in an application, we process it, get the transcripts of your grades from your college, then review everything for possible enrollment. As you can see, it's a—"

"But I want to start classes on Monday," Josh interrupted.

"I'm afraid that's impossible, sir."

"Well," Josh grinned, "I *tried.*"

Actually, he felt relieved. Now he could go over to U.C.L.A. with a clear conscience. He could enroll in law school knowing it was "God's will." He knew fully well that he was engineering the situation, though. He was telling God that he would go into Christian work if he could get accepted in this seminary today, and he knew when he went in that it would be impossible.

To ease his conscience, Josh decided to give it one more try. "Who is the head of the school?" he asked the woman at the desk. "Who's the last person I'd talk to if I took my problem up the ladder?"

"That would be Dr. Charles Feinberg, dean of the seminary," she said.

"Is he in?"

"In the summer, he almost never comes in to the office," she told him.

That's great! Josh thought, but said nothing.

"However," the woman continued, "today he *did* come in. I'll see if he can see you."

Dr. Feinberg waved Josh into his office and pointed to a chair by his desk. The dean was obviously engrossed in a serious writing project. Books and papers were spread out on his desk. He did not seem to resent the intrusion, however.

Josh approached his desk and sat down. He decided to be completely honest.

"Sir...to tell you the truth, I don't *want* to go to seminary." He briefly explained the events of God's persistent call and his own evasiveness. He told him about Dr. Halverson's invitation and his running away. "I can't explain it, sir. I guess, deep-down, I want to trust God with my whole life. But I'm also afraid to give up my own plans and goals. I suppose none of this makes any sense to you, does it?"

It was impossible to tell if the dean was really listening. Dr. Feinberg had been sitting there as Josh talked, sometimes looking out the window, other times looking at Josh.

The man stared outside a long moment and asked what seemed to be a totally unrelated question, "Is that your car?" He pointed to the small MG sports car in the lot outside.

"Yessir," Josh replied.

There was another thoughtful pause. The silence was long enough for Josh to begin to feel uncomfortable. Then Dr. Feinberg spoke again.

"What were your grades like at Wheaton?" he asked, still looking outside.

"They were good," Josh answered.

Again a silence. Finally, Dr. Feinberg turned and said, "Young man, call Wheaton College. Tell them to send a transcript of your grades. Have it sent airmail. Then fill out an application. You'll start classes Monday."

Josh's heart sank. *What am I getting into?* he asked himself.

There was no way of getting out of it now. His "bargain" with God had been specific. "If I can enroll today, I'll know it's Your will," he had prayed.

Although he had resigned himself to attending classes at Talbot Theological Seminary, Josh seemed to be doing so against his will. His attendance and performance were mechanical, perfunctory.

For more than a month he simmered over the decision. Everything he had struggled for during four years of college was wasted. His dreams were smashed. Why was God so capricious? Why couldn't Josh simply be the Christian attorney he felt motivated—more than anything else in his life—to be?

CHAPTER
EIGHT

"Ask McDowell, he seems to be the expert."

The statement and his name interrupted Josh's reverie in Dr. James Christian's *Church History* class. The professor looked at Josh and smiled, knowing he had caught the student day-dreaming.

Instead of letting the remark pass, however, Josh slammed his book shut and jumped up. "That's it!" he cried out. "I've had it with this theological 'cemetery'!" He threw his books down on Dr. Christian's desk and stormed out of the room before a stunned class.

He pushed through the door in anger and ran to the street to get away. A block from the campus he slowed to a walk. It was exactly 11:45 and the lunch recess bell rang at the junior high school building he was passing. The sound startled him and he stopped suddenly. Josh backed against a telephone pole on the sidewalk as the junior high building erupted in pandemonium. Kids seemed to pour out of the building pell mell in what seemed to be an unending stream.

Josh pushed himself against the telephone pole and seemed paralyzed. The hundreds of running, yelling students rushed in every direction. They kept coming and coming. The entire building was emptied in less than a minute, but to Josh—frozen in place—it seemed to last much longer.

He was surrounded by excited and happy junior high students who were oblivious to anything but the moment.

Unable to move, Josh simply stared. It seemed that God's voice came to Josh in that moment in unmistakable clarity. *Josh—I've called you to reach young people. Do not turn your back on it.*

Josh was both startled and reassured. That God would address him so specifically surprised him. But the sense of inner peace that He gave with the declaration greatly calmed his fears and put everything into its proper perspective. Never before had he experienced such a supernatural sense of God's presence and purpose.

It's true. God does want me in Christian work. As long as Josh could be that certain, he would not worry about law school. He could close the door on the past and trust God for the future.

He went back to Dr. Christian's class and sheepishly apologized for his actions. The incident became the pivotal point for his involvement at Talbot.

Dr. Robert Saucy, another professor, noted the new sense of seriousness with which Josh now approached his work. It was refreshing as there was a new attitude prevailing on this as well as other Christian campuses. It was a by-product of the so-called "hippie" influences emerging in both the counterculture and in Christian circles. It was the anti-intellectual, experiential bias toward all of life. "I don't want to study theology and philosophy," was the way the argument went, "just give me the Bible. I just want the Bible."

"Having a heart for God is commendable," Dr. Saucy reflected, "but if evangelicals want to gain ground on the same basis as non-evangelicals, they have to have a heart for biblical scholarship."

"Yes, sir," Josh acknowledged.

"You seem to have that attitude, Josh—you're not afraid of intellectual approaches."

"I guess that's why I'm at seminary instead of law school, Dr. Saucy," the student replied.

"It's a good decision. Even if God leads you into law at some future time, this preparation is invaluable. The war won't be won only on a spiritual basis. There will be battles on an intellectual level."

"That's true," Josh observed. "That's how I was won to Christ at Kellogg College—through intellectual inquiry."

"Well," Dr. Saucy smiled, "remember that the reverse is equally true. You can't convert a man only on an intellectual basis. The spiritual must be present for balance."

Dr. Saucy became more than a professor to Josh. He was a friend. Josh was drawn to the man's convictions and learning. He in turn, a normally reticent man, liked Josh's outgoing ways and eagerness to share his faith with strangers.

Once, when they were going to a ball game, their car was stuck in the traffic jam inching toward the parking lot. By the time they reached the entrance gate, Josh had engaged the driver in the car next to them in conversation, explained the four laws concept to him, and guided him in a prayer to receive Christ! Dr. Saucy happily rejoiced with Josh in his excitement. To the professor it was audacity; to the student, something natural.

Dr. Saucy told him, "Josh—I've always had a fear of sharing my faith. I've often been hesitant. But you make it seem easy. You're a breath of fresh air."

Josh formed a small organization from which to direct his weekend speaking engagements. He called it "Focus on Youth" and began to acquire names for a mailing list.

Dr. Saucy heard about the plans and said to Josh, "Look, my wife and I want to help. As a family project, my wife, our three children and I will take the responsibility of putting out your prayer letters. We'll maintain your mailing list. I've got an old Gestetner machine to make the metal address plates. The kids want to help. We'll fold the letters and see that they get mailed."

"That's great, Dr. Saucy," Josh smiled. "That means a lot to me."

Josh had taken to a special Bible verse and used it often in his new ministry. It seemed to more accurately characterize his life than anyone else in the seminary at the time. No one had a greater boldness or energy in witnessing for Christ. The verse was typed on a card over his desk:

> *"For I am not ashamed of the gospel of Christ:
> for it is the power of God unto salvation...."*
> *Romans 1:16*

God's power had the capacity to change lives. While Josh wasn't always able to follow up those whom he led to Christ, he did stay in touch with many. From these experiences came a certain "excitement of the unexpected."

George was a 20-year-old student on the campus of a nearby community college. While sharing the four laws and the gospel with George, Josh learned he had just been released from jail on serious drug charges. After listening attentively to Josh, his eyes filled with tears. He grabbed Josh's arm and said, "Man...that's what I need. I want to receive Jesus."

After prayer and further conversation, Josh got up to leave, promising to stay in touch with George. A short time later George went into the student center to find Rick and Carlos, two of his friends.

"Guys," he told them, "I'm off the 'stuff.' I think I've really got myself together."

"What d'you mean, George?" Carlos asked.

George explained his encounter with Josh and how he had prayed to receive Christ.

"What are you doing, man?" Carlos snapped. "Are you *crazy?*" The three of them had not only been heavily involved in drugs, but were part of a Satan-worshipping cult of over 100 people on campus. They were openly dedicated to destroying the principles of Christianity.

"I'm not crazy," George told them. "In fact, for the first time in my life, I found one thing that really makes sense."

Not only was George's testimony powerful to his two friends. His completely transformed life also spoke loudly and clearly.

Some time later Carlos was arrested and taken to court on narcotics charges. It was an open and shut case, a bench trial. Carlos heard none of it. As the prosecutor argued, his attorney bargained and the judge pronounced his findings, all Carlos could hear was the testimony of George calling him to conversion.

Carlos called on Josh at Talbot Seminary when the trial recessed. "Man, I don't even know how it's going," he told Josh about the proceedings. "I mean, the judge can sentence me to a hundred years and I could care less. I just know I gotta get right with God. I had to come by and see you."

Josh prayed with Carlos upstairs in the faculty lounge while several fellow students were downstairs praying for Carlos. When Josh explained the third spiritual law—that Jesus Christ was God's only provision for man's sin, Carlos was convinced. He prayed to receive Christ. Next he went through 16 days of withdrawal from drugs "cold turkey," which amazed everyone. God's power was great enough to give him the miracle of beating his drug habit without cramps, nausea, hallucinations and other desperate physical side effects usually associated with withdrawal. Carlos also saw God work another miracle. The judge provided leniency on the

CHAPTER
EIGHT

drug charges and he was spared from a jail term.

When George and Carlos both became believers, the power of their transformed lives got to their friend, Rick.

Businessman Robert Seelye was speaking on the subject of the resurrection and giving his testimony at a campus meeting put on by a Christian group where Josh was also helping.

Rick, "high" on drugs and half-crazy, came into the meeting. Red-eyed and disheveled, he ran toward the speaker screaming curses and spitting in Robert's face.

Josh ran over and grabbed the intruder and slammed him against a blackboard in the classroom they were using. "Listen, mister," Josh said sharply, "if you had any guts at all, you'd go home and check out who and what you're damning. In fact, I challenge you—go home and read the third chapter of John six times. But before you do, ask God to show Himself and His Son, Jesus, to you. I dare you to do that—but now, get out of here." He steered the raging student toward the door.

This was Tuesday. On Thursday, Josh was back on campus for a meeting. He went to shut the classroom door when a foot jammed into the doorway. Josh looked to see it was Rick.

Josh became defensive and didn't want a repeat of Tuesday's incident. "What do you want?" he asked.

"Well...I...wh..." the student seemed to have lost his fury. "I took you up on it. I went home and called another guy from the Satan cult to be with me. Well, we both prayed that prayer—about being open to God—and began to read John 3 six times. But we only got through it four times when we both felt God there in my room. We both gave our lives to Jesus."

It was another obvious example of God's power at work in changing lives. Rick was excited about his new life. "What do you call this religion?" he asked excitedly.

"It's not religion," Josh explained. "It's knowing Jesus personally. It's Christianity."

The conversion of three of its top members had a profound effect on that cult of Satan worshippers. They had vowed to cripple or frustrate Christianity in the community. It appeared, however, that their efforts were neatly neutralized and the teeth of their threats muzzled. They saw that the Satan they had worshipped did not have omnipotent power.

Josh's excitement over conversion was always fresh and genuine. During the week, between classes, he'd witness for Christ on nearby campuses, at shopping malls, gas stations, wherever he went. On weekends, he traveled—mostly in southern California—representing his ministry, "Focus on Youth."

One night following a "Focus on Youth" crusade, Josh returned to the Talbot dorm about 10:30. He parked his car and locked it. As he turned toward the dorm, he suddenly felt as though he was caught in a vise of some force. It squeezed his chest, pushing the air from his lungs. All he could manage was a feeble, stifled cry as the paralysis forced him to collapse. Josh panicked. He could not breathe or even move. His eyes rolled toward the back of his head.

Providentially, someone coming out of the dorm at that moment saw him fall. He was fortunate. No one would have heard him cry out.

Josh heard someone yell, "Call an ambulance—I think he's having a heart attack!"

He was able to gasp shallow breaths every now and then through extreme concentration and effort. Josh felt as if his heart had been stopped by complete paralysis. Never had he experienced such crippling, intense pain. He prayed that his body would somehow be able to breathe until help arrived because he knew that he was slipping into unconsciousness.

Josh woke up in a rescue squad van racing to the hospital. A paramedic was giving him oxygen.

"It's a good thing we were able to answer the call," he grinned at Josh. "An ambulance wouldn't have gotten there in time. You're lucky."

The doctors in the Buena Park hospital emergency room administered a muscle relaxant which seemed to release the grip on Josh's heart and lungs. He was able to breathe a little bit on his own while they tested to see what was wrong.

As Josh reflected over the incident, he remembered only a sudden tearing, squeezing, suffocating feeling. He could almost imagine satanic glee over his helplessness.

CHAPTER
EIGHT

At first the medical men thought Josh had fallen victim to spinal meningitis. They kept the flow of oxygen going while they checked. "There's been an outbreak of epidemic proportions on nearby military bases," a doctor told Josh. "If it is spinal meningitis, we'll have to quarantine you. It's a deadly serious disease."

"I...appreciate...your encouragement," Josh whispered hoarsely.

The doctor took a spinal tap—a painful process—and sent the contents of the vial to the lab for study.

It was nearly three in the morning when one of the doctors came into the room. "It isn't spinal meningitis," he said. "That's the good news. I guess the bad news is that we don't know exactly what your problem is. Are you feeling any better?"

"A little," Josh answered. "But I feel so weak."

The doctor checked his pulse. "We'll want to keep you under observation."

"The pain," Josh said, "the pain was terrible. Here...in my chest."

The doctor nodded. "My guess is that it was a spasm of the myocardium. Very rare. Probably just a one-time thing." Then he asked Josh about his family medical history—did his father have a heart problem? Did Josh have rheumatic fever or measles as a child? Was this his first encounter with such an incident?

When the doctor was satisfied that Josh was going to be all right, he released him into the care of a student friend who had followed Josh to the hospital.

"Make sure they put you into the college health center," the doctor ordered. "We want to keep you under observation for a few days. Plus, bed rest is the only thing to help put you back your feet."

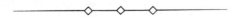

Dr. Charles Feinberg was among those who came to visit Josh in the college health center. Josh loved the man almost as much as his own father. They were about the same age, but the similarities ended there. His father was an earthy, simple farmer. The dean of Talbot Seminary was a man of quiet introspection and aristocratic dignity. Josh was probably

JOSH

the only person who could get away with being casual or flip with the man.

While all the other faculty members were on a first name basis with one another, no one would dream of calling the dean anything but "Dr. Feinberg."

Perhaps that is why Josh was more or less surprised to see him at the end of his bed.

"Dr. Feinberg," Josh smiled, trying to smooth the covers and feel more presentable.

"McDowell..." the older man acknowledged. "How are you?"

"Okay, I guess. It sure was a scary thing, though."

"So I hear. Are you comfortable here?"

"Yes sir, I—"

"Anxious to get back to the books, though, I suspect."

"Yes, but I—"

"I know—you're worried about those mid-terms. Well, we'll work out something—perhaps you can make them up on a Saturday." Dr. Feinberg had the habit, irritating to Josh, of anticipating him and finishing the statement for him. One time Josh was in a meeting with the dean when he did that to Josh. Exasperated, Josh blurted at the time, "Dr. Feinberg, if you'd just *listen* a minute, you'd get things straight."

Silence had suddenly descended on the room then. The dean had looked at Josh and said in measured tones, "All right, Mr. McDowell. I am listening. Now...what is it you're trying to say?"

Josh now recalled that incident with a smile. He was glad to see Dr. Feinberg and told him so.

After a period of conversation and prayer, the dean stood up. "Josh," he said quietly, "when you're well enough to leave here, I want you to come and live with my wife and me."

"Sir?" Josh asked.

"My wife and I want you to be, well, sort of our 'adopted' son—live in our home. Would you do it?"

"Sir, I think that would be fantastic."

One month later, just before Christmas, Josh got an

CHAPTER
EIGHT

emergency call telling him his father had died. He scraped together all the money he had and flew back to Michigan for the funeral.

He conducted the service and spoke briefly at his father's funeral. "Dad's life has been brand new these past 14 months," Josh said to family and friends gathered before the casket. "Dad has spent the past 14 months witnessing in prisons, giving his testimony and sharing his faith. He also took time to renew a father-son relationship and even in the space of just a little over a year, spent quality time with me and established for me the kind of father role that I will want to give to my son some day."

There was no way to undo past damage to his body, however. Josh's dad finally collapsed and died because of the earlier destruction of his liver.

"But one thing was always on Dad's mind," Josh told the mourners. "He wrote me a letter before he died telling how he witnessed to different people in town—how he wanted them to have the deep peace and power that he found." Josh took the letter from his pocket and read it to those listening. One by one, as they heard their names mentioned, they looked down or shuffled nervously.

" 'I talked to Owen at the hardware store today,' Dad wrote me, 'and Owen said Jesus was fine for me, and maybe one day he'd consider coming to Christ—but not just now. Son, I sure hope he doesn't wait as long as I did to give his heart to Jesus. Pray with me for Owen, and Sam Mc-Clennan...' "

Josh did not read the letter to embarrass his listeners, but to show them the love his father had for their eternal well-being.

When the funeral was over, Josh spent time with his brothers and sisters and settled the family estate matters. Then he called on Jeannie.

"I'm sorry about your dad, but glad he's in heaven," she told him.

"Jeannie, I just came by to say in person what I've already told you by telephone and letter—"

"Josh," she said, touching her fingers to his lips. "Please—don't say it."

She looked at him, eyes wide and pleading.

JOSH

"Couldn't we try again?" she asked.

"I'm sorry," he said. "I'm just not in love...."

"But you loved me once—I know you did. You'll get the feeling back. I'm willing to wait if you'll try again. Please...won't you try?"

Josh shook his head. "Jeannie...I'm sorry for the crummy way I've handled things. I mean, running away and not dealing with it. But things won't change. I'm sorry."

He released her hand. "Good-bye...." he said as he closed the door.

CHAPTER NINE

BACK IN CALIFORNIA JUST AFTER CHRISTMAS, Josh had time for much introspection as he waited for classes to resume after the holidays. The thing that seemed to preoccupy his mind most was triggered after his dad's funeral.

"I often think how unfair life is sometimes," he had told his older brother. "Dad had such a complete transformation of his life that I wish Mom could have shared in it with him."

That was the thought which he considered now. It was great that Dad died a Christian—but wouldn't it have been wonderful if they could have experienced the joy of knowing Christ together before they died?

Then Josh thought of his mother. She had such a deep respect for church and the Bible. He wondered why she had never become a believer. No doubt her self-consciousness about her appearance—or perhaps her husband's drinking reputation—kept her from church. But what kept her from trusting Christ?

Josh was depressed to think about heaven without his mother. Yes, he was glad Dad would be there, but how could he look forward to it if she were not there?

The more he thought about it, worried about it, the more depressed he became. Finally, he was unable to sleep or study.

Was she a Christian or wasn't she? He had to know. But how? It was an impossible request. "Lord," he prayed, "I don't even know how to pray about this. But You know that I'm miserable. I can't eat or sleep. All I think about is whether Mom died as a believer or not. I *have* to know, Lord. Somehow, give me the answer so I can get back to normal. Please," Josh pleaded, *"I've just got to know!* I can't live the rest of my life without knowing one way or the other."

Two days later, he drove his small MG to Manhattan Beach, mostly to clear his head and get his mind off his obsession. The weather was pleasant for January, so he parked the car and decided to walk out to the end of the pier.

Several people were fishing, but he all but ignored them. Any other time he would be eagerly sharing Christ and chatting with them. He was too depressed to talk to anyone now.

Josh looked off the end of the pier into the dark water.

"It's too cold to go swimmin' with all your clothes on," a voice teased from some ten feet or so away.

Josh turned and smiled. The voice belonged to a woman who looked like someone's grandmother.

The woman was sitting in a lawn chair fishing. She was bundled in a thick woolen sweater and wore a battered old hat to screen her face from the sun.

"Yeah, I guess it would be too cold to go swimming," Josh remarked.

"Well, you were gettin' so close to the edge I thought you were gonna jump in."

"No...I guess I was just day-dreaming," Josh said, then added, "Are the fish biting?"

The old woman pointed to a bucket at her feet which contained a half dozen or so small fish.

The woman was friendly and soon had Josh engaged in lively conversation. "Where are you from?" Josh asked her. "Hardly anyone in California was born here."

"I know what you mean," the woman laughed. "We're from Idaho originally. Where's your home?"

"Michigan," Josh answered, "a little town called Union City."

"Union City, eh?" the woman squinted.

"Nobody's heard of it. I usually tell people it's a suburb of—"

"Battle Creek," the woman interrupted.

Josh was surprised. "You've heard of it?"

CHAPTER
NINE

"Yes—I had a cousin from there. Did you know the McDowell family?''

Josh blinked at the woman. There was only one McDowell family in town.

"Wilmot McDowell—they had five youngsters."

"Yes," Josh said smiling, "I'm one of them—I'm Josh McDowell."

"You're fooling me—"

"No, I'm Josh McDowell! Wilmot was my dad."

"I can't believe it!" the woman exclaimed. She introduced herself as a cousin to his mother. "My name's Bowder now. But I was brought up with your mom and dad in Idaho. When he was young, your dad used to haul watermelons over the mountain pass to market."

Mrs. Bowder asked Josh why he was in California and he told her about attending Talbot Seminary.

"Oh, I know about Talbot. We've had some gospel teams from there at our church. We go to Community Baptist Church," she said.

"You do? How long have you been a Christian?" he asked.

"Oh, a long time. Most of my life, son."

"Mrs. Bowder—do you remember anything at all about my mother's spiritual background?"

"Why, sure." The woman's eyes squinted again as she stared out to sea, recalling old memories. "I sure do remember. Your mom and I were just girls—teenagers—when a tent revival came to town. Your mom and I went every night. It was quite a big thing for our small town. Exciting," the woman recalled. "Then—I think it was the fourth night—we both went forward to accept Christ."

"Praise God!" Josh shouted. The neighboring fishermen turned to look, then went back to their own business.

Josh grabbed Mrs. Bowder's hands and squeezed them. Her fishing pole clattered to the pier deck and he clumsily grabbed it before it fell into the water.

"Mrs. Bowder, you are an answer to an *impossible* prayer!" he exclaimed, telling her about his Thursday request of God.

The two talked for nearly two hours before exchanging addresses and telephone numbers. Josh agreed to visit her home afterward.

Driving back to the seminary was a test of Josh's powers of concentration. He had to check himself several times as the small MG approached the speed limit. All the way back Josh kept thanking God for such a fast answer to his prayers.

It was to him such a specific answer to prayer that he knew God would never have set up the circumstances so miraculously to let him know about his mother's decision if, in fact, the decision were not genuine.

Tears of joy ran down his cheeks as he thought of the reunion his parents were having in heaven.

Dick Day was also a student at Talbot. He had become a Christian at age 28 after becoming a successful businessman. As a result, he started his seminary training much later than most students.

Dick, his wife Charlotte and four youngsters lived in a small apartment just off campus.

He and Josh developed a friendship, their common affinity no doubt based on their similar secular backgrounds. Josh also saw in Dick a father figure, and often came to him for counsel.

Dick had joined the staff of Campus Crusade for Christ and told Josh about the work, encouraging him to come on staff with him. Josh told Dick about meeting Bill Bright while he was a student at Wheaton College and Bright was on campus recruiting.

"Well, we're not many yet," Dick smiled, "only about 50 or 60 people. But we're growing."

"Maybe," Josh said. "I'll think about it. But the reason I came to see you tonight is to ask your advice about a problem I have."

"Sure, what is it?"

"Well, my brothers and sisters are upset with me because I've been telling about my dad's drinking and what I did—before we were Christians. They said I'm airing dirty laundry in public and it's nobody else's business. They're really irritated at me. But every time I share our testimony of

CHAPTER
NINE

how God dealt with my hatred and brought us both to Christ, it has a tremendous impact and power. Do you think I'm wrong to talk about my dad like that in public?''

Dick thought for a moment. Then he asked, ''Do you share anything that your dad hasn't said in public concerning his background or conversion?''

''No...I don't think so,'' Josh replied.

''Then I don't see anything wrong.''

Josh grinned. ''Thanks, thanks for your help.''

''Remember,'' Dick called after Josh, who was already at the door, ''remember to pray about joining the staff of Campus Crusade.''

Whether it was original with him or someone else, Bill Bright was quoted as saying, ''A man's strength is very often his weakness unless it is controlled by the Spirit of God.''

Josh had a ''holy boldness'' which he knew some had already mistaken for arrogance or brashness. The only way people would be able to discern that it was not brashness or arrogance was to live what Bill Bright referred to as a ''Spirit-controlled'' life. Josh had followed that principle since Bright shared it with him at Wheaton that day. Whenever the principle was tested, it was because of a lack of maturity or wisdom—both of which would come in time. What mattered was the consistency of that Spirit-filled and Spirit-directed life style.

Dave Nicholas was the right example to Josh of that principle in action. Dave was a popular speaker and musician, known all over southern California. Yet, for some reason, Josh knew only that he played the trombone and was an experienced song leader. No one mentioned to him that Dave Nicholas was also a topnotch youth speaker.

A lesser person, without that right attitude and spirit, would have been too proud to do what Dave did. Josh asked Dave if he would direct the music and play in his ''Focus on Youth'' meetings while Josh spoke. Dave was a much better speaker than Josh, but said nothing. He happily agreed to cooperate. This relationship would continue for two years before Josh learned Dave was a better youth speaker than himself.

Josh was impressed with Dave's Christlike qualities. If Dave had advice or criticism, Josh welcomed it, because he knew it was prompted by the right character.

"Josh," Dave said to him one day, "I've been listening to you for the past several weeks and I think you're going at it wrong. You're preaching on sin so hard that *you're* trying to convict people. That's the job of the Holy Spirit. Let God do the convicting. Expose sin and then tell them about God's love."

Josh was inspired by reading missionary biographies. His heroes were Jim Elliot, Nate Saint, John Paton and Hudson Taylor. It pained him that there seemed to be such a void in the contemporary world of similar leadership qualities. He was determined to try and model himself after their lives.

He read accounts of how Hudson Taylor and others of his heroes rose at 4:30 in the morning to spend time with God in prayer and Bible study. He tried to set the same pattern in his own devotions.

It lasted three days.

Then he recalled that a hundred years earlier there was no electricity. In the days before electric lights, people went to bed at eight o'clock at night, when it started to get dark. Josh was often traveling to speaking engagements or appointments, on the go until one or two in the morning. No wonder he had difficulty getting up at 4:30 to pray.

The lesson he learned was not in keeping to their schedule, but to their faithfulness. His own quiet time schedule was different, but it became a habit. He found it to be just as effective for him at eight in the morning as Hudson Taylor's was at 4:30. What mattered was that you met with God each day.

At his quiet time each morning, Josh prayed about the challenge of Dick Day to work with him among college-age young people. Ever since he had met Bill Bright, and had watched Campus Crusade in action in Illinois, Josh had been impressed with the organization. They seemed to be the most biblical of the groups he knew about. Campus Crusade also had a strategy—they knew where they were going and had a plan to get there. They had a commitment to the local church as a means of evangelism for them, not as a threat or competing organization. Josh also admired the quality of staff people as much as he respected Bill Bright's leadership.

Certainly he wanted to work with college students. But where? How? Should it be with Campus Crusade?

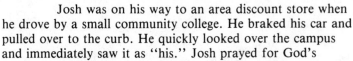

Josh was on his way to an area discount store when he drove by a small community college. He braked his car and pulled over to the curb. He quickly looked over the campus and immediately saw it as "his." Josh prayed for God's leading, but knew when he first saw it that the Lord wanted him to begin Campus Crusade work there at Cerritos Community College.

Dick Day, his friend and fellow student at Talbot, was Orange County Coordinator for Campus Crusade. He agreed to appoint Josh to be student staff director at Cerritos and the work began at once.

Josh got permission to leave certain classes five minutes early and arrive late for others by five minutes. This gave him a full hour between. He parked his MG near the classroom, tore out from the class early, roared off in his car, shared Christ with several people, and hurried back for the next class.

Josh was incredibly energized by seeing such a practical relevance in his studies. As he learned some new theological or spiritual truth in class, he often saw a chance to use it in action the same day. Some mistook his zeal, however. They thought Josh was boasting or putting them down because they weren't witnessing as he was.

Even Dick Day had troubles at first. Josh reported to Dick as his superior. When weekly reports were turned in, Dick reported one convert—Josh reported ten. The next week, if Dick had ten reported conversions, Josh had 50. There was no "catching up." The problem was a barrier that Dick created, however. Josh was oblivious to any competition. It took several months of this before Dick could put the problem in perspective. He discovered that each man had differing spiritual gifts—just as Paul and Barnabas. The name

JOSH

Barnabas means "son of encouragement." He was determined to be a Barnabas to Josh.

Josh had been dating frequently while a student at Talbot. He preferred to date many girls rather than get serious about any one, however.

One girl he met was a new Christian. Cathy had been first runner-up in an international beauty pageant and had all the physical endowments and personality qualities of a winner. Cathy and Josh dated each other almost exclusively for the month they had known one another. Cathy seemed to have everything—beauty, talent, clothes, money and a wonderful family. It was her mother who answered the phone one evening when Josh called. "Could I speak to Cathy?" he asked her.

"Just a moment, Josh," her mother said, "I'll get her."

She was away from the phone for just a few seconds when Josh heard a scream on the other end of the line. In another instant, Cathy's mother was back on the phone. "Josh! Come quickly!" The woman was nearly hysterical. "It's Cathy!" she cried. "She's trying to kill herself!"

Josh sped to their house. Cathy and her mother were both crying when he went inside.

"What's wrong, Cathy?" he asked.

The young woman looked away, still weeping.

"She won't tell me anything," her mother said finally. "Do you think she should have a doctor?"

"No! I don't need anyone," Cathy stormed.

"Cathy," Josh said quietly, "tell me what's wrong. Why would you want to—" he paused, hoping she would respond.

"Come on," he said. "Let's go for a drive. You'll feel better." Josh glanced at Cathy's mother who nodded.

Cathy did not resist when he lifted her out of the chair and draped a sweater over her shoulders.

In the car they drove along while Cathy slowly began her story. Soon a confession poured out of her.

"Josh," she cried, "I'm pregnant!"

"But, how...who—"

CHAPTER
NINE

"It happened before I met you. I was a new Christian and I got involved with _____." She named a prominent church youth worker. "He told me that there was nothing wrong with sex, so we went to bed together several times. He broke it off the night before I met you—but not before he made me pregnant," she cried bitterly.

"Oh, Josh," she sobbed, "what can I do? I thought it had ended. The reason I went out with you is because I wasn't afraid of you. You never made any physical or sexual demands of me."

Cathy began to sob so hysterically that Josh was afraid she'd choke. He drove her back to Dick and Charlotte Day's house and convinced her that they would help.

Charlotte tried to comfort Cathy while Dick took Josh aside for counsel.

"What should we do?" Josh asked.

"We? I thought you said you haven't touched her," Dick said.

"I haven't, Dick."

"I know. I only said that because when you said 'we' you seemed to already be involved with her problem. Josh...listen. It's *her* problem. Not yours—*yet.*"

"What do you mean?"

"Don't you see? Something like this could *ruin* you. How long would you last in the ministry if people even *thought* you were the guilty party."

Josh saw the implications, but he knew he couldn't abandon the girl either.

Dick and Charlotte prayed for Cathy and for wisdom to know what to do. Then Josh drove her home.

The next morning Josh told Dr. Feinberg about the problem and asked for his counsel. "Don't see her again!" he said.

Josh retreated to his room to pray. He was honestly as concerned for Cathy as he was for his own ministry. He could not sacrifice her to save his own reputation.

"Lord," he prayed, "if You have a ministry for me, then You'll have to protect it and guard my reputation. I believe that the right thing to do is help Cathy. I can't turn my back on her."

The answer came after two weeks of prayerful

consideration. Josh found an evangelical home for unwed mothers in another California town and made arrangements for Cathy to move there until the baby was born. They confided in Cathy's mother who agreed with the decision.

When the baby was born, it was adopted by a Christian couple whose own prayers were answered.

CHAPTER TEN

SEMINARY CLASSES HAD ENDED FOR THE SUMMER when Dick Day came by Talbot to look for Josh. He wanted to talk to him about joining Campus Crusade as a student director.

"I can't," Josh told him.

"Why not?"

"I've thought about it," Josh explained, "but if I joined I'd have to be at Arrowhead by the middle of July, right?"

"Training starts July 20," Dick nodded.

"But I've got an entire summer lined up with a speaking tour. I have 'Focus on Youth' meetings until the start of the school year," Josh explained.

"Well, at least pray about it," Dick suggested.

"Okay...I will."

Josh told the Lord, basically, that if it was His will for Josh to join the Campus Crusade staff, He would obviously have to act in such a way as to work out the scheduling dilemma. Josh did not feel he could cancel any of the meetings at such a late notice. He left on tour as planned.

The trip called for him to travel to northern California, to Oregon, Washington, Idaho, Montana, and across several other western states to Minnesota, then down through the Midwest.

Josh started out with all kinds of faith and practically no money. He drove the first week to several small churches in northern California. Disappointingly tiny crowds turned out, most of them young couples. He knew they were least likely to be able to help because of their own economic hardship. Despite this, Josh gave his best effort. He preached

JOSH

from Proverbs—"He that winneth souls is wise." The offering each evening was barely enough for Josh's modest meals. He slept folded up in his MG. But one church, in San Jose, with one such small crowd of young couples came to Josh late at night. "We don't know why," the spokesman for the group said, "but God laid it on the hearts of several of us couples to take another offering for your work. There were only a handful of us—I wish we could do more, but—here— take this with God's blessing." Inside the envelope was $600 to be used for his trip expenses. Now he could sleep in a cheap motel, stretched out in a bed, instead of cramped in his car.

When Josh got to Seattle where he had scheduled a week of meetings at a Christian and Missionary Alliance church, mail and messages caught up with him.

When he returned all the telephone calls, and read the letters and telegrams, Josh could not believe what had taken place. A flurry of cancellations—one church had a schedule conflict, another had a pastor leaving, one was in financial difficulty. The reasons were all different, but the result was the same.

All his meetings scheduled for *after* July 17 were cancelled!

He took this as the obvious sign that the Lord wanted him to go with Campus Crusade, and went on to complete what remained of the tour.

In Helena, Montana, Josh was scheduled to speak several nights at a small church where about 50 people came to hear him. It was the first time he had spoken where genuine, spontaneous revival broke out. The entire congregation—including the speaker—was overwhelmed with a sense of sin and the need for repentance. Josh led the congregation in what turned into a three-hour service of praise, confession and prayer.

At the next meeting, the same thing happened, but the crowd had grown to nearly a hundred. By the final meeting, there were 200 in the congregation and God moved significantly in many lives.

As an indication of their gratefulness to God, when the offerings were taken for Josh's work, the small church generously contributed nearly a thousand dollars into the

CHAPTER
TEN

offering plates. However, when Josh was ready to leave that week for his next engagement, the pastor gave him an envelope. Instead of the love offering promised, there was $25 in it.

Trip expenses had used up his other money by this time. All he had was the $25 to get him to Minnesota where he was scheduled to speak.

After carefully estimating how much money he would need for gas for the two-day trip, Josh figured how much he'd have left for meals—about $2.00. He stopped at a grocery store and bought a loaf of bread, a jar of peanut butter and a jar of grape jelly. For the next two days he'd eat sandwiches and sleep in his car again.

After driving a full day, however, Josh got an idea. He stopped in a small town in North Dakota and knocked on the door of the parsonage of an evangelical church.

"Pastor," he said, "my name's Josh McDowell," and explained his dilemma. "I'm wondering if you could put me up for the night?"

"Well, I dunno," the minister hesitated. "How do I know you're who you say you are?"

Josh showed the man some identification and literature with his photograph along with materials from his speaking tour.

"Well," the minister said, "I guess it'd be all right. Come in."

"Who was it, Harold?" a woman's voice called from another part of the parsonage.

The minister ushered Josh to the parlor where the woman was sitting. "This young man needs a place to stay. I told him we'd let him stay in the spare bedroom."

"What?" the woman asked sharply. "We'll do no such thing. This isn't a mission."

"B-but," the minister pleaded, "he has no place to go."

"No. Absolutely not. We don't know anything about him. We don't even know who he is."

"I checked his driver's license. And these brochures have his pictures on them. I believe he's all right."

"Harold." The woman was obviously used to getting her own way. "That person is *not* sleeping in this house.''

Josh was embarrassed and totally at a loss for words. Finally he managed to stammer, ''Is it okay if I sleep on the floor of the church?''

''Well, of course,'' the minister smiled.

''Harold—remember the new carpet. He can't sleep on the new carpet. Let him sleep downstairs.''

Josh spread some large pieces of cardboard on the concrete floor of the musty basement of the old church. He realized too late that he'd have been more comfortable sleeping in his car.

The next day, Josh left for Minnesota.

Despite the discouraging setbacks with his most recent church experiences, Josh had not become cynical. For this, God seemed to bless. At the Evangelical Free Church where he spoke at a series of services, many trusted Christ.

At the conclusion of the series of meetings, the pastor stood up. ''Friends,'' he told the congregation, ''Josh has really ministered to us this weekend. Let's take up *another* offering for him.'' Following his experience in Montana, Josh half-expected to be handed only a few dollars.

But *all* of the nearly one thousand five hundred dollars was given to Josh. It was enough to get him back to California and provide for his campus ministry expenses for several months.

Following the successful ministry at the Minnesota church, Josh had three days to drive back to Arrowhead Springs in time for the staff training. He stopped only long enough for short cat naps, otherwise drove straight through.

As soon as he returned to California, Josh was to go to Arrowhead Springs, near San Bernardino. Campus Crusade for Christ had acquired the property about a year earlier. Each summer, the organization provided staff training for new recruits as well as seminars for those who had been on staff for over a year.

Dick Day had promised Josh a scholarship to attend the sessions in July. He was eagerly looking forward to the seminars and training opportunities.

As he was getting situated at Arrowhead Springs,

CHAPTER
TEN

Josh happened to look out the window. His eyes widened in disbelief as he saw someone walking by outside. Josh ran to the window and threw it open. He yelled at the man passing by to wait.

Tearing down the stairs and running outside, the two men grabbed one another in a bear hug.

"Dick Purnell! What are *you* doing here?"

"I was going to ask you the same thing."

The two roommates from Wheaton College enjoyed a laugh-punctuated reunion.

"I thought you were off to law school," Dick grinned.

"And I thought you were in medical school."

"I guess God spoke to each of us separately," Dick observed. "I was at a Campus Crusade training session in Minnesota when I felt God calling me to turn down my medical school scholarship and get some theological training at Harvard."

"Pretty much the same with me, I guess," Josh told him, filling in the highlights of the time since their graduation from Wheaton.

The two enjoyed their reunion and the time spent together in various training sessions at Arrowhead. Then it was time to go back to their respective schools and get ready for the next academic year.

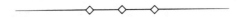

As Josh considered how he could work with Campus Crusade while attending seminary, he knew he'd have to have financial help.

He reasoned if he could find 25 friends who would help by investing $5 a month, he could do it.

Josh went to a pastor friend and explained the idea. "I've made it my 'fleece'. If the Lord wants me to take this assignment, He'll help me find enough people at $5 a month to cover my expenses. Will you pray with me that God will show me what to do?"

Rev. Enoch Moore looked at the young man on the other side of his desk. He saw an intensity and maturity to be encouraged. He reached into his wallet and pulled out a $20 bill.

"I want to be first," he told Josh. "Put me down for $5 a month."

The other 24 supporters came to him almost as quickly. Thus prepared, he looked forward to the work on campus in the fall.

In addition to directing a Campus Crusade work at Cerritos College, Josh taught a class in leadership training at Fullerton Junior College.

Of the 17 Christian college students in this class, he had first noticed a pretty young freshman coed.

Paula Simpson had also noticed Josh. She sat in the back of his class and sometimes didn't hear everything he said. Instead, her own thoughts had intruded.

He's really good-looking, Paula told herself. *But he's so old. I'll bet he's at least 24 or 25. Probably even married.*

After the class, Paula was on her way out when Josh stopped her. "Hi, I'm Josh—what's your name?" he smiled broadly.

She returned his smile, and to him the entire room lit up. He had noticed her eyes at first—wide, brown and expressive. But now he was won over by her smile. She was absolutely stunning.

"I'm Paula...Paula Simpson," she said, somewhat shyly. Even her voice was attractive—musical, bright—with no trace of stridency.

"Glad to have you in my class," Josh said after an awkward pause. He was still holding her hand from a handshake that lasted just a bit too long.

"Thank you. Well, I've got to go to class now. Nice to meet you," Paula smiled.

Paula Simpson, Josh remembered the name.

The next week, at a Campus Crusade meeting, she was back—along with 384 other Fullerton students. At first Josh had a difficult time spotting her, then he saw her. His eyes stayed on her and several times he caught her glancing his way.

"Now, as you know," the student leader was telling the group, "this is our first *big* meeting of the school year. And, as I told you when you first came in, a Crusade staff member, Josh McDowell, wanted to do something special.

*CHAPTER
TEN*

That's why he had you fill out those 3 x 5 cards with your name on them. You see, we've put those 3 x 5 cards into this big basket and Mr. McDowell is going to pull out the name of a winner. That lucky person will win the door prize—three Saturday night dinners with Josh.''

There was a buzz and *ad lib* wisecracks as the student stirred up the cards and held the basket high over Josh's head.

Josh reached in and pulled out a 3 x 5 card. He handed it to the student who read the winning name into the microphone.

"Paula Simpson is the winner of three Saturday night dinners with Josh McDowell!''

Josh did not tell anyone that he had spent the better part of the afternoon writing the name "Paula Simpson" on nearly 400 3 x 5 cards. Nor did he mention that he had taken the cards of the others and dumped them in the other room and came back with his supply of cards for the drawing.

The next three Saturday night dinners stretched into a chain of succeeding dates as well. Although Paula was not yet 19, she seemed to have the maturity and Christlike values of a woman much older. She had a soft-spoken beauty and spiritual radiance that were communicated through her pleasant personality. She was not only beautiful, but intelligent and gifted—fun to be with.

Josh was equally attracted to her parents, Don and Vivian Simpson. Paula's dad was a college administrator and active in their church. When Josh met Paula's mother, it was obvious from whom Paula had inherited her good qualities.

The Simpsons were beautiful people—and excellent role models for Josh as to the kind of marriage he wanted. If he could have the kind of love and marriage relationship that Don and Vivian had, he would be happy.

Paula had a twin sister. Leslie was dating a young man named Paul Lewis. Paul and Josh got to know each other quite well since they often crossed paths at the Simpson house.

Josh was a man with enormous energy and drive. Never content to do one thing at a time, he always had work with him—whether on a date, a social outing or other occasion.

JOSH

Don Simpson marveled at Josh's capacity to do several things simultaneously. He would be busily engaged in conversation with Paula, reading a book for school and taking notes for an assignment, and setting up meetings by telephone. He juggled all without missing a beat.

What amazed Don was that Josh even occasionally stole a glance at the football game on TV—keeping abreast of that action as well!

It seemed Josh had a telephone growing out of his left shoulder, attached to his ear. He conducted a lot of business by telephone, much of it by long distance.

Sometimes, during lulls when the operator was trying to locate someone for him, Josh would talk to her as if she was a long lost friend.

"How are *you* today?" When the operator responded, he would light up and with a smile which was communicated in his voice say, "Say, did you know that God loves you?"—and went on to witness to her.

The telephone also allowed Josh to go where he might not otherwise be able to.

"We need a van for our campus work," Don had heard Josh tell Paula and Leslie. "It's the only practical way to get our teams from one campus to another. We need a van."

Don Simpson watched as Josh searched through his notebooks looking for various numbers, then called one.

'Hello, Walter?—well, is Walter there? I'd like to speak to Walter," he told his party. After a brief pause, Don heard one side of the conversation, which began, "Hello...is this Walter Knott?"

Knott, well-known because of his *Knott's Berry Farm,* was also famous as a southern California philanthropist. How Josh got his personal phone number as well as an answer was a puzzle to Don Simpson. Josh went through a brief but clear presentation of their need and why Walter Knott was the one person who could help. In the end, Josh got his van.

At first, Don Simpson thought that quality of Josh's was brashness. He came to learn, however, that Josh simply expected everyone else to be as generous as he was. As a Christian, Josh had said, people were expected to give if they were able.

Vivian Simpson had seen Josh demonstrate the principle several times over in his own life. Once he came over wearing just a light T-shirt. He had literally given "the shirt off his back" to a needy hitchhiker he had picked up.

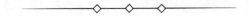

It seemed as if the entire Simpson household was under siege in December. It was Josh's senior year at Talbot and his thesis was due January 4.

Normally it took the better part of a year to produce a thesis. Dr. Saucy had been lenient to Josh because of his "Focus on Youth" speaking ministry and Campus Crusade work at area colleges. Those assignments alone were equal to a full-time job. Seminary studies occupied another great portion of Josh's time. In addition, he had moved into the home of a prominent family, babysitting for them to offset his room and board.

Now, however, it was time for Josh to give total concentration to his thesis. The best place for that was in the Simpsons' living room. Josh checked out dozens of books and periodicals from the library and began to read and take notes. It was an intensive project that went nonstop until Christmas.

Josh researched, read and wrote continuously until he collapsed from lack of sleep, usually on the living room floor. Then, after a few hours' nap, he'd pick up his papers and start again.

Don Simpson saw the scope of Josh's project and shook his head. "It would take me two *years* to write that thesis," he told his wife. "He thinks he can do it in two weeks. And the crazy thing is—I think he can, too!"

When Don came home from school administration meetings, Josh was usually hard at work, papers spread all over the floor, piles of note cards on the sofa, books piled on the coffee table. It was hard to find a path across the room. He had to pick his steps carefully.

Mrs. Simpson was enlisted to type the thesis for Josh after he wrote it.

In the end, the enormous project was completed and turned in on time. The subject consisted of an examination of

the Jehovah Witness' position on the deity of Christ. The
work was given an *A* by Dr. Saucy.

A minister complained to Josh about his use of the
four laws—now in booklet form—which Josh used in many of
his witnessing encounters.

"I don't use the four laws," the minister said,
"they're too pat and not biblical."

"Not biblical?" Josh echoed. "How can you say
that? Look at John 3:16. For God so loved (law one) a sinful
world (law two) that He gave His only Son (law three) to
'whosoever' believes in Him (law four). The entire Bible
reflects these principles," he told the pastor, adding, "Look
at the first three chapters of Genesis—God created a world
and man and has a plan for us to share to His glory...law
one. The rest of the Old Testament tells us how man became
sinful and separated from God...law two. The Gospels tell us
about Jesus as the answer...law three. The epistles show how
to make personal application...law four."

Josh told the minister how the four laws booklet
was being used by God's Spirit to convict and convert hundreds in his town alone. "It may not be perfect, but it sure
beats what most people use—which is nothing."

"Yes," the minister admitted. "I must confess that
you're right."

The four laws booklets were being used by the
thousands by Josh and college students across Orange
County.

George attended a meeting at Fullerton Junior
College and was led to Christ. His assignment as a new
believer was to present the four laws to three people and get
their reactions.

George's wife was one of the three. She prayed to
receive Christ and was given the same assignment. She
presented the four laws to four counselors at the boys' home
where she worked. Three of the four attended a lay institute
meeting with George and his wife and were converted. They,
in turn, went with a group to the beach, witnessed to people,
and led four others to Christ. In two weeks, all but the most
recent "generation" of believers in the chain were trained to

CHAPTER
TEN

reproduce.

The four laws booklets *worked* and it was never difficult to get people to use them as a witnessing tool once they had worked for them.

A deep love had been developing between Josh and Paula over the year they had been dating steadily.

If he had been cautious about becoming serious with a woman after his broken engagement with Jeannie, such fears were groundless. The reason he backed away from marriage with Jeannie was that he simply did not know if he loved her.

With Paula, it was different. Now Josh knew. Dick Day and other happily married friends had repeatedly told Josh when he'd ask how he'd know if he was in love.

"Oh, you'll *know,* all right," they assured him.

It was true.

Of course, it went beyond mutual attraction or compatibility. Yes, they both enjoyed Mexican food and the same music. Their spiritual values were the same. They were comfortable with each other. Despite all this, there was a magical, mystical quality which bonded them together.

Because of her studies and his ministry, the couple had few private times where the two of them could relax together. Most often it was to flop in front of the TV in the den to watch a movie. Or, once in a while, they were able to drive to the mountains or beach and watch the sun go down.

At such times, Paula would cuddle next to Josh, his arm around her. They chatted for hours about everything important to them. And they prayed. These were beautiful, totally joyous times.

Prayer together brought greater intimacy to their relationship. Their growing love for one another was expressed in lingering embraces and warm kisses. However, because Paula's prayers and attitudes seemed to bring him closer to Christ, Josh could not bring himself to take advantage of her in those remote and romantic places.

There was an almost unspoken agreement between them. Whenever they sensed pressure of the moment or feelings of arousal, it was not at all uncommon for one of them to gently break away and say, "Well, maybe we'd better head back."

Nor was it at all uncommon for one of their dates to be cancelled, changed or interrupted because of Josh's work.

Paula, if she resented being left out or separated from Josh at some ministry-related occasion, never showed any irritation. It was obvious to her, though, that she was not the only person in Josh's life. In fact, she often felt as if she were the *last* person.

Josh phoned her one evening before a date. Such a call so near the time he was to come was sometimes begun: "Honey, I'm running a little behind schedule. I may be late."

"How late?"

"Three or four hours."

There were other times when such a call simply prefaced a change in plans. Tonight was one of those situations.

"Honey, is it all right if someone comes along on our date tonight?"

Paula laughed, "Who is it this time, darling?"

"Well," Josh began to explain, "I picked up this fellow on the highway. He doesn't speak any English. He hasn't had a bath in *days*—maybe weeks. I brought him to the dorm and put him in the shower...gave him some clean clothes...and led him to Christ."

"And now he needs something to eat, so wouldn't it be nice if we took him to dinner?"

"Uh...yes. Yes," Josh said. "Is it okay?"

"Of course, darling. Bring him along."

Paula hung up the telephone and smiled. There was no way she could be angry with Josh. His ways were innocent. *Besides,* she thought, *it's all right if I share him with people now. If—when—we get married, I'll have him more to myself.*

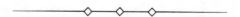

Dick Day and Josh planned one of the most monumental evangelistic efforts ever conceived for the student population of the southern California area. They called it the Balboa Beach outreach.

*CHAPTER
TEN*

Scheduled for the week of Easter, they planned to use Christian college students from the Orange County area to be trained and go out on the beaches to witness to some 50,000 university students on the beaches during the spring break.

Nearly 200 Christians had been thoroughly briefed on sharing Christ.

The plan called for special meetings, featuring illusionist André Kole, to be held in a nearby ballroom. It was packed out every evening. So was the supper club and coffee house which they had also rented.

In fact, so many people were coming to the Campus Crusade meetings that the local bars seemed empty by comparison.

A university fraternity had set up a "watering hole" called "Socrates Den" across the street from the Christian activities. There was a banner across the building housing the Campus Crusade work. It said, *"Christ is the Answer."*

The frat beer-drinkers put up their own banner above Socrates Den. It proclaimed, *"Booze is the Answer."*

A *Los Angeles Times* reporter and photographer happened to see the sign. The paper carried a feature on the activities and mused, "Which will win, Christ or booze?"

Paula, her sister, Leslie, Paul Lewis and Josh—along with scores of other students—invaded the beaches to share Christ with the collegians.

At the coffee house, one of the fraternity leaders from Socrates Den came over to mock.

"Hey, anyone here have a beer?" he called out.

"Yeah—come on in," Dick Day greeted him. Dick took him aside and poured him a root beer. "On the house," he grinned. Then as the young man sat drinking the root beer, Dick asked him if he'd ever heard of the four spiritual laws.

By the time he finished his root beer, Dick had led him to Christ. He went back across the street and told what happened, and three other fraternity men came over, curious.

Josh, Dick Day and others talked to them and all three prayed to receive Christ.

The pattern continued until about half of the 15 or 20 mockers who were sent over became Christians after checking things out.

At the end of the week the *Los Angeles Times* carried a postscript to their feature. It was headlined: *"Christ Wins."*

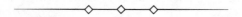

Laguna Beach was another target of witnessing. Dick Day, Hal Lindsey, Josh and other Crusade staffers had trained and organized some 250 key Christian college students. They met for two hours of Bible study, prayer and final instruction at a nearby church. Then they left, all 250 of them, marching six abreast down the street toward the central beach in downtown Laguna.

It was a time of growing campus unrest and summer strife, so the authorities were understandably nervous when the march began.

People ran out of the stores lining the route.

"What's going on?" they asked.

"Here, let me show you," someone would say, dropping out of formation to talk to them about Christ.

The "parade" had by now grown to about 400 as people followed to see what was happening.

Police cars sped past the marchers to direct traffic ahead of them. The authorities were relieved to learn that the "mob" was a Christian student group with peaceful motives.

At the beach, all 250 students lined up shoulder-to-shoulder, a huge line of young people carrying the clipboards and the campus survey sheets designed to open up the opportunity to share the four spiritual laws. At the signal, all 250 headed for the nearest "sun worshipper."

"Hi...I'm Josh, and I'm here with a group—"

"Yeah, man! I *believe* you. What's goin' on?"

The Laguna Beach encounter accomplished its purposes. Several thousand people heard the Gospel message, and hundreds prayed to receive Christ.

CHAPTER ELEVEN

JOSH

DICK DAY HAD CALLED JOSH AND TOLD HIM THAT BILL BRIGHT WANTED A MEETING WITH THE TWO OF THEM.

They drove to Arrowhead Springs and met with Bright who got right to the point.

"Josh, you can't go on giving half your time and allegiance to Crusade, and half your time and loyalty to 'Focus on Youth.' Either God has called you to work with Campus Crusade for Christ or He's called you to your own work."

"I thought I'd be able to keep them in balance, sir," Josh explained. "This past school year I spent time on campus during the week, and went out for speaking meetings on weekends and during the summer when school is out."

"It's better that you choose now, Josh," Bright explained. "I know from experience that eventually you'll be forced to decide between them. It's better to choose now and focus all your energy on that choice so you and your ministry can be maximized. It's the only way."

"I see...."

"Josh," Bright continued, "Dick has told me that you're graduating from Talbot with highest honors. Well, that's exactly the caliber of men we're looking for at Crusade. But it can't be half and half. Pray about it—and let me know what God tells you to do."

"Thank you—I will."

Several days later, after difficult prayerful consideration, Josh called Dick Day to tell him he had decided to give up "Focus on Youth."

"It was hard," Josh admitted. "I really like speaking and want very badly to become a speaker."

"Well, don't give up," Dick told him. "I believe God gives us the desires of our hearts when we commit ourselves to Him, when we leave choices to Him."

"You mean I might get to speak for Crusade? But I thought Crusade already had a speaker."

"We do. And he's good. But the way I see the work growing, one man—ten men—won't be able to keep up with the opportunities," Dick said.

Josh was eventually assigned as a Canadian director at the University of British Columbia. He would be leaving for the assignment as soon as summer staff training was completed.

One day he got a telephone call from elsewhere on the grounds of the Arrowhead Springs facilities. "I want you to come up here right away," a man on the other end ordered. Josh hung up the phone, wary of the edge in the voice he heard. He went up to the man's office who quickly ushered him in and shut the door. The man was obviously upset.

"I heard a rumor today that disturbs me greatly and I wanted to clear it up before it gets any farther."

"What kind of a rumor?" Josh asked.

"Someone told me that you told them you were talking about being a speaker for Crusade."

"Yes, if God leads—"

"Listen," the man interrupted. "Crusade already has a speaker for university campuses. That's *me!* You will *not* speak. There's only room for one speaker in this organization. No one else will ever get a chance to speak, so don't ever *plan* on it! Do you understand?"

In this rough and troubled atmosphere, Josh knew it would do little good to try to explain the reasons he felt called to give up his speaking ministry and come to Crusade. Both Dick and Bill Bright had encouraged him that he might one day be used as a speaker here.

"This is *my* ministry—my territory. Don't forget that!"

The meeting had a chilling effect on Josh and made him a little bit cynical about the "human-ness" of some

Senior guard, Josh McDowell, enjoys district championship honors
with Union High teammates.

sh was a halfback and
ebacker on the Union City
gh school team.

An Air Force recruit in 1957, in the
Dover, Delaware base barracks

Josh graduated from Union City High School in Michigan in 1957.

Prior to a European speaking tour while a student at Kellogg College, Josh and a friend organized the Superior Painting Company and painted houses.

Josh with his father, Wilmot, about a year before his death. Josh's neck brace was the result of whiplash from an auto accident.

During a three-month 1965 speaking tour in Mexico, Josh poses with the interpreter, soloist and others who coordinated the meetings in Mexico City.

Speaking at a dual Guatemalan and Mexican youth convention near the border, Josh stops with his interpreter and singer.

The men in Josh's Action Group for discipleship during his campus ministry at the University of British Columbia

Josh takes the free speech microphone on the University of Illinois campus in 1970. An audience of hundreds listened.

The first time the Auburn University free speech area was ever used, Josh was there.

At the University of Alabama, Josh speaks in the free speech area.

An animated Josh speaks on Maximum Sex to more than 5000 students at Louisiana State University.

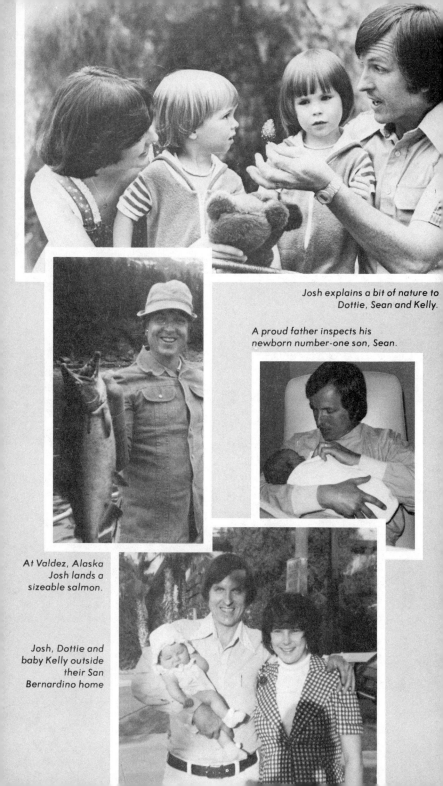

Josh explains a bit of nature to Dottie, Sean and Kelly.

A proud father inspects his newborn number-one son, Sean.

At Valdez, Alaska Josh lands a sizeable salmon.

Josh, Dottie and baby Kelly outside their San Bernardino home

Microphones crowd the platform as Josh lectures to a large indoor university audience.

JOSH IS HERE

JOSH IS COMING FEB. 20-21

DON'T MISS JOSH

Enthusiastic students on campuses everywhere creatively promote Josh's speaking appearances.

Handbills by the tens of thousands have helped spread the word.

JOSH IS COMING

PROPHECY

While visiting campus, Josh is frequently invited to be a guest lecturer in university classrooms.

Josh clowns with Mark Lundeen, research coordina...

Josh addresses a speech audience at University of South... Califor...

Creative campus publicity has attracted hundreds of thousands to witness Josh's famous dating pantomime, a part of his Maximum Sex lecture.

Josh married Dorothy Ann Youd on May 22nd, 1971 at Foxboro, Massachusetts.

Exposure to huge crowds has never dampened Josh's enthusiasm for personal interaction with students and laymen.

Because of his campus impact, Josh is frequently interviewed by representatives from local newspaper, radio and television media.

Josh enjoys
a quiet moment
with Dottie.

The McDowell
children: Katie,
Kelly and Sean

CHAPTER
ELEVEN

people involved in Christian work.* He said nothing about the incident.

"Lord," Josh prayed later after reflecting over the incident, "if You ever give me a speaking ministry, I pray I'll have an attitude of sharing—and not be threatened by others who want to do what I do."

At the University of British Columbia, Josh wrote a letter to Paula. Now a college junior, she had transferred to San Diego State University. They were over 1300 miles apart and missed each other desperately. Their telephone calls and letters expressed this fondness. Both were busy, however, so loneliness was not too terrible for them.

Josh wasted no time in setting up a Campus Crusade work in British Columbia. Vancouver was located just a short drive north of Seattle on Canada's southwest coast. Patterned after his work at Cerritos College, Josh soon had an active student group involved with the Crusade ministry at the University of British Columbia. The university was not unlike a major U.S. college. Students came from a number of Canadian cities. Many were also foreign students from Europe, Latin America or Asia.

Joseph Krieger was the son of a prominent Jewish businessman from Great Britain. The Krieger family had strong contacts in Israel, but the young man had come to Canada for his education. Joseph, along with a contingent of several other young Jewish students, came to one of Josh's Crusade meetings with the idea of disrupting the service.

Before they had a chance to break up the meeting, Josh began to speak. His topic was prophecy and the young men found his talk fascinating.

The next day, Joseph barged into Josh's office on campus.

"Listen," he said to Josh sharply, "send everyone away! I've got to talk to you."

---

*The speaker would prove to be his own undoing, however. The man and Crusade parted company some time later. It was apparent to Josh that God had taken His supernatural blessing away from the speaker.

JOSH

Josh's student leaders quietly left the room and Josh waved Joseph to a chair, at the same time extending his hand.

"I don't believe we've met," he smiled. "I'm Josh."

The student was obviously troubled. He sat down and got right to the point. "I heard you speak last night," he said. "And I want to know two things—first, what does it mean to know Jesus Christ personally, as Messiah? Secondly, how can my life have an impact on the world?"

The young man was a serious student and had been touched by Josh's talk the night before. Josh and Joseph talked for nearly nine hours in the office. At the end of their dialogue, Josh invited Joseph to become a Christian. The young man prayed to receive Christ.

He later wrote to his family and his rabbi, sharing the details of his conversion. Joseph joined the staff of Campus Crusade and served for a year before going back to England, "to win my father to Christ," he said.

Josh also lectured at the University of Calgary at Alberta. In the audience was a young Hindu from India. He had been in the country just six months and knew almost nothing about Christianity. But as he listened to Josh's lectures over three evenings, the truth began to break through to him.

As the final meeting broke up, he went forward to talk to someone about becoming a Christian, but all the counselors seemed to be busy talking to others. The young Hindu could find no one to talk with. So he went to the most quiet spot he could find—the men's room—and went to a corner. After reflecting over Josh's invitation, the man quietly prayed to receive Christ.

The next day, a Christian student approached him. "Have you ever heard of the four spiritual laws?" the student asked the Indian. He invited the Christian to sit down and explain it to him. When the student got to the law explaining the chasm between God and man, the Hindu spoke up excitedly, "Yes—but Jesus Christ did something about that!" When the student got to the prayer, he asked, "Wouldn't you like to receive Jesus Christ into your life?"

The Indian student grinned, "Ah, but I have already done so." He explained what had happened the previous evening.

CHAPTER
ELEVEN

Paula had been thinking about Josh. Lately her mind had been more and more on him. And on the subject of marriage.

At Christmas Josh had driven back for the holidays and she had come home. They were glad for the time together and noted that their love for each other—if anything—had grown stronger because of their separation.

Paula also noticed that Josh was just as involved as ever with his many projects. He was on the telephone constantly at her parents' home and rushing madly from one appointment to another. Several of their dates were spent in the company of Crusade staff people or church group.

She was getting used to Josh's "life in the fast lane"—as someone aptly described it.

Paula wondered about the kind of marriage adjustments such a life would dictate. She had already changed quite a bit. Josh believed in her. She had been shy and reserved. He had encouraged her to speak, to give her testimony at retreats, conferences and other meetings. He gave her plenty of encouragement and consistently built up her self-esteem.

He had also helped her develop spiritual qualities. Paula was grateful for Josh and his helping her become the woman she was turning out to be.

Before the holidays were over, the two of them had discussed their plans for marriage again.

They went to Paula's parents and asked their permission to marry.

Don Simpson was impressed by the gesture of respect, but said, "That decision is really yours. We love you both. I think it's a great idea. But it's an important decision. Pray about it."

"We have, Daddy," Paula said. "We both want to do what God tells us."

"And we can't see any reason why He wouldn't have us do so," Josh added. "But Crusade has a policy about staff members getting married. They can only do so at certain times of the year." This was to preserve continuity in their ministry during the school year. "We want to get married this summer, Lord willing."

JOSH

At Easter break, Josh arranged for Paula to fly up to British Columbia to spend a week there.

The time they spent together was enjoyable and refreshing. It was exciting and fun to be with each other and do things as a couple.

They talked and prayed long hours together and planned aspects of a life together. Their prayer was simple, "Lord, we really want to make our marriage part of Your will. We want Your blessing on our plans." When they kissed good-bye at the airport, they were both nearly in tears. So deep was their love for each other that it was almost impossible for them to separate. "Oh, Josh," Paula cried, "we were meant to be *together,* not apart."

Back in San Diego, Paula remembered their prayers for God to make their marriage part of His will. Is that why the past few days she had been restless, not at ease with her thoughts about Josh and marriage?

She couldn't put her finger on it, but something gave her a distinct lack of peace. Perhaps it was the restlessness of his life that gave her troubling thoughts. Even now he was planning a crusade to Latin America. *From Canada to Latin America to where?* she wondered. *His life is a constant merry-go-round. Can I live with that kind of life? I'm home-oriented,* she thought. *I don't think I could travel at his pace. Oh, God...what should I do?*

For the next several weeks, Paula had a sensation of a terrible knot in her stomach. She had trouble eating, sleeping and concentrating on her studies.

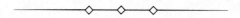

Josh did not call Paula for almost three weeks after their time together. As soon as she left he had his work which occupied most of his time. But that wasn't why he hadn't called.

The fact is, Josh wasn't sure why he couldn't talk to her now. It was strange. As soon as she left, he began to have haunting doubts about marrying her. At first he thought it was just a case of the jitters following the broken engagement years earlier with Jeannie.

*CHAPTER
ELEVEN*

There was no reason to back away from marriage now. Josh was absolutely certain he loved Paula. There was no doubt in his mind at all. Nor did he question Paula's love for him—or her obvious qualities. She was gorgeous, intelligent and fun, to be sure, but her beautiful Christlike character was probably the greatest attraction to him. She was loving, honest, communicative and supportive.

I probably am where I am now because of Paula as much as any other person, he reflected.

It was logical, then, that they should be married. *Then why am I being plagued by doubt?* Josh wondered.

Because she is not the right woman.

"Where did that thought come from?" Josh asked aloud.

She is not the right woman for you.

"What kind of nonsense is that, Lord?" he prayed. "She's the woman I *love.* I *want her.*"

No.

"But why, God? Why would you take someone so wonderful away from me? Where have I sinned?"

Josh began to bargain with God—to be somehow more spiritual if He would only give Paula to him.

In the end, he gave up struggling. He didn't understand it at all, but knew that he had to go to Paula and—he couldn't even form the thought, it hurt so badly—cut off the relationship.

Paula put her robe on the bed, sat down in front of her dressing table and was brushing her hair when her roommate came in.

"Hey, I hear Josh is coming," she said to Paula. "That's super!"

Paula was pulling the brush listlessly through her long brown hair and staring at her image in the mirror.

"I thought you'd be all excited," her roommate said. "Is something wrong?"

Paula put down the brush. "I...I'm going to have to tell Josh that I can't marry him," she said. "We're going to have to break up."

"But I thought you loved Josh!"

"I *do,*" Paula sighed. "That's what's making it so difficult."

"But if you love him, what's the problem?" the roommate asked.

"I...I don't know. I just know that God won't give me any peace of mind over this."

"I don't get it," the girl shrugged.

Paula smiled. "I'm not sure I do either."

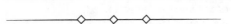

Josh picked Paula up at her dorm and kissed her warmly before she got in the car. He drove to a quaint Mexican restaurant, one of their favorites.

Both sensed something between them and were unusually quiet as they drove to the restaurant.

After ordering from the big menus, Josh waited until the waiter walked away, then said, "Well...what do you think?"

Paula immediately began to weep--"Oh, Josh, I feel awful," she cried.

Her tears got to him. He began to cry also. "Honey...for some reason," he stammered, "God won't let us go ahead with this."

"I *know,*" she cried, "I feel the same way."

"I didn't call you because I didn't want to hurt you."

"Me, too," she said tearfully.

They ate without fervor and said little.

Josh pulled out her chair and said, "Let's go down by the water...maybe drive to Balboa Park."

They felt more freedom to talk as they walked outside in the night air. As they talked, retelling and reliving old memories, it was obvious they would be giving up good times past and future.

"I don't understand," Paula said, shaking her head. "Are we stupid?—what's wrong?"

"I don't know," Josh answered. "Maybe," he considered, "maybe we should go ahead anyway. We love each other. Maybe that's all that matters."

"We both know better than that," Paula reminded him. "This has to be of God—and if we fight Him, we'll both

CHAPTER
ELEVEN

be miserable and lose His best for our lives.''

"I feel like I already have lost the best thing in my life,'' he muttered.

"Look,'' she reminded him, "we were going to get married this summer. Let's wait until summer before we write the relationship off.''

"All right,'' he agreed.

"Let's just go our separate ways. If God wants us back together, He'll show us by the end of summer.''

That is the way it was left. They would get together at the end of summer and—well, see what would be next.

As they continued to recall pleasant memories of the past, both expressed their gratefulness that neither had given in to a sexual expression of their love for one another. It was the one satisfaction of a deeply emotional struggle.

The next morning as Josh left for the airport, he put on a false front of exceptional bravado. He kissed Paula good-bye for what he knew would be the last time and walked through the door of the rampway to his flight. He had smiled and waved, his stomach wrenched inside him and he felt like vomiting. Tears streamed down his face as he made his way through the aisle to his seat.

He had never experienced such grief. He hesitated before sitting in his seat—wondering if he should run back and shout, "Paula, I love you! Let's get married.''

If he had, she probably would have run to him and shouted, "Yes!''

As the plane began to taxi away from the terminal, Josh engaged in angry dialogue with God.

"God, how could You be so unloving, so uncaring?''

All things work together for good....
"Good? This isn't good. It *hurts!*''

I didn't say doing My will wouldn't hurt. Only that it would work for your good. Remember, I will withhold no good thing—

"What? What about Paula? She's the best thing to ever happen to me.'' Then the thought came to Josh which made sense of it all. "Then...the woman You will give me will be *better* than Paula?''

Not better than Paula...but better for you than

JOSH

Paula.
"Then You're not angry at me?—punishing me?"
No. I want only the best for you.

CHAPTER TWELVE

THOUGH HE HAD PEACE FOR THE TIME BEING ABOUT
PAULA, Josh's spirit was still suffering. He was a seminary
graduate, but he had been with Campus Crusade for four
years and had never taught a seminar at a conference. All he
had ever done was take care of the book table area and make
sandwiches, etc., for those who were witnessing. Have you
ever made one thousand sandwiches? And have you ever put
the Four Spiritual Laws booklets inside the sandwiches with
the peanut butter? He just didn't feel appreciated—Campus
Crusade didn't realize what they had.

Then, suddenly, his hour of glory came. He got a
call from Ted Martin of Crusade's Institute of Biblical Studies
to teach at the IBS meetings later that year! He couldn't
believe it—he had gone from nothing to everything, all at
once.

He prepared thoroughly for nearly six months. He
planned to teach a series from the book of Romans and when
it was nearly time for the IBS meetings, had a wealth of notes
and materials. He was looking forward to this speaking
ministry.

A week before he was to leave for IBS, Josh got a
phone call from Bill Bright in California. "This is a special
year for us at staff training at Arrowhead," he said. "It's our
international year and we'll be having the largest staff ever.
Josh...the administration at our hotel has fallen apart. I need
you to come back here and help me. Please make
arrangements right away. I'd like you to be back here in three
days to take charge."

There was a pause on Josh's end of the line. He had
been looking forward to teaching at IBS. *What an abominable*

JOSH

sense of timing, he thought. *I don't want to go!*

"Josh, I need you," Bright repeated.

"Okay...I'll be there," he said and hung up.

Angrily, Josh threw his clothes and books together and packed them into his car. He fumed all the way to California, and his attitude was no more pleasant when he arrived.

His assignment was to supervise the 30 staff people and organize the facilities for the nearly 1,700 people from all parts of the world.

Josh stayed up all night the first few days trying to put together procedures and organization.

He tried to establish a basic administrative plan to handle the logistics of the hundreds of internationals expected.

An inexperienced staff of 30 was no match for 1,700 incoming people—many of whom had trouble with English. Some had customs regarding meals and housing which were at odds with the best-laid plans of Josh and his people.

To make matters worse, the hotel's equipment would break down, but never when it was convenient. Only when it caused further disruption.

Finally, the proverbial straw. A terrible case of dysentery broke out. The sickness spread in a matter of two or three days to just about everyone. There were lines at every rest room, which were overworked to the point of breakdown also.

Josh found himself—with bucket, mop and toilet plunger in hand—making the rounds of the rest rooms. The rest of the staff was either out sick or tied up with the needs of meals and other chores.

Josh himself was sick, but had no time to think about it. Every toilet in the hotel and other buildings had to be scrubbed twice a day. He was working 20 to 22 hours a day, able to catch only cat naps of two or three hours a night.

Somehow it all got done. But Josh had not been able to attend a single meeting to hear any of the world-famous speakers brought in for the occasion. He did meet one of them, however.

He had just finished with the toilets on the second floor and filled his bucket with fresh water. He picked up the plunger and started down the stairs to the lobby.

*CHAPTER
TWELVE*

There he ran into Bill Bright escorting Billy Graham on a tour of the facilities. "Oh, Dr. Graham," he paused, waving to Josh, "I'd like you to meet our Canadian director, Josh McDowell."

The tall evangelist smiled graciously and stuck out his hand.

Josh awkwardly stuck the plunger under his arm, took the bucket in his left hand, wiped his right hand on his shirt and sheepishly shook hands with Billy Graham.

As they walked away, Bill Bright remarked, "You know, our staff people are devoted. They're willing to do anything."

Josh wanted to shout after them, "I'm *not* willing!"

The next morning Josh nearly lost his temper when an assistant to Bill Bright stopped him.

"Those plastic flowers by the front desk are dusty. I'm sure Bill wouldn't appreciate it if he came by and saw they were dusty. You ought to dust them," he told Josh.

Josh imagined doing something else with the plastic flowers, but got out a rag and dusted them.

In the afternoon, the brand new red carpet was finally vacuumed in the lobby. It was the last chore Josh had to do before he could finally go to hear one of the speakers. At long last he'd be able to participate in one of the meetings which had been going so well. Then Bill Bright rushed up to Josh.

"Come here—quickly!" he called to Josh. The parking lot had just been tarred and someone had obviously walked in it and tracked in the thick, tacky tar. His footprints were visible across the length of the lobby. "Get something— some cleaner, some rags. Hurry and clean it up before it sets," Bright said.

It took all afternoon and most of the night to clean up the tar. The more cleaning solvent he rubbed into each spot, the bigger it got. It called for more scrubbing, hard scrubbing.

A Crusade staff person came by just as he was finishing and teased him.

"Scrub harder, slave. I still see some spots." He was joking, but Josh was obviously in no mood for humor. He was ready to throw in the towel—rather, rag. Angrily he stood and was all set to heave the solvent can at the front desk, to be followed by an extremely vocal resignation. Somehow the urge was checked.

A sudden conviction came over him. No one was really out to get him. He had brought the attitude of bitterness with him from Canada.

Josh recalled with feelings of repentance the Scriptures he had read in devotions that morning describing how Jesus washed the feet of the disciples. Immediately the thought came over him, "If Jesus can wash their feet, why can't I scrub their floors and clean their toilets?" It was an immediate lesson in submission.

The Bible illustration seemed to burn into his spirit, all the more convicting because of the Lord's example and his nasty attitude.

That night Josh prayed for grace to be a true servant for Christ. He realized that before you can ever become a leader you need to learn how to be a follower. And the next day, Josh began a new pattern of service. He went out of his way to find things that needed doing; he worked harder and later than anyone else. It was something he *wanted* to do as a service to Christ, to make up for getting off on the wrong foot. For the next several weeks he scrubbed harder and cleaner to learn submission.

The spirit was not lost to others. Bill Bright told Josh, "God can teach us many things in a servant's role. When we first started, there were so many valuable things I learned by washing dishes, planting flowers, mowing the lawns—and yes—" he laughed, "even scrubbing latrines!"

It was a difficult time as Josh continued the back-breaking work of taking charge of the six-week international staff training. Because of the work, sleeplessness and sickness, Josh had lost over 20 pounds.

There was difficulty also in measuring his progress in his quest for submission and acquiring the attitude of a servant.

His first question was—*What can a person learn through being a servant?* Was Bill Bright merely trying to sound spiritual by indicating God teaches through submission?

Sure, the Lord said, "The greatest shall be the least," but wouldn't it be better to use your abilities for God in an aggressive, leadership capacity? Josh thought the church

CHAPTER
TWELVE

was lacking capable leaders and wondered if it was right to constantly put himself in that subservient role.

Everything he heard from Christian leaders, plus what he read about the subject in the Bible, all pointed to that earlier conviction—that God honors the servant and promotes the one who defers to others.

It would be a lesson to consider again and again, not one easily learned.

Bill Bright had been criticized by some outsiders who claimed he had his hand on too much of Crusade's operations. When the organization was small, it was both possible and necessary for him to be involved in every detail. But now that it was growing, they reasoned, he should begin to delegate more responsibility to his assistants.

Bright was committed to building a quality organization and concerned about time running out before the task of global evangelism was accomplished. He had a vision for Crusade being used of God to literally take the gospel message to the entire world—not just through student and university outreach, but also through evangelistic efforts involving cities and nations.

Hard at work on these concepts, he was unaware at the time that there were a few on his leadership staff who were more committed to strange dogmas and ideas than to Bright's original vision. They saw Crusade in a totally different light—as itself a church or denomination, rather than an organization devoted to *helping* the church.

Some of these leaders wanted to share these strange concepts with the new students recruited for staff positions.

Josh, having been assigned to be administrator of the summer training program, refused to give them the time. "These young people are very impressionable. A lot of them are new believers," he told them. "I can't let you teach them your ideas. They don't have any part of the Crusade philosophy."

"You can't do this."

"Yes, I can. I have the authority. If you want to go to Dr. Bright and have it changed, I'll cooperate. But, for now, I'm responsible and I say no. You can't speak to the summer staff."

Soon after this incident, it was "placement time"— when personnel placements were considered and assignments given out.

Josh had been promised an assignment worth waiting for. To him it was the ultimate "plum." He would be assigned to work under Carl Wilson in the high schools, to travel across the United States as a speaker. He was delighted, too, because working with Carl on high school campuses would not make him compete with the other coordinator who had earlier shouted that Josh would never speak in Crusade— that it was his territory.

He had all but forgotten that incident, as well as his encounter with the leaders who had wanted him to allow them to speak to his summer staff. Thus denied, they had consulted and found a way of dealing with Josh.

A regional director called Josh in to discuss his placement. "We're sending you to Argentina," he said.

"Argentina?" Josh echoed. "But I thought—"

"I know you were planning to work with Carl Wilson. But there seems to be some question about your loyalty to the team. Going to Argentina will prove you're an organizational man," he said.

"But Argentina," Josh observed. "That's about as far away as you can send somebody."

"Well, either you go...or leave staff," the director offered.

"I'll go," Josh said simply. He knew he had been called to Campus Crusade for Christ. He knew God didn't call him to an organization that had perfect leadership. But they were his leaders.

In his studies on submission, Josh had come across a verse in Hebrews 13: "Obey your leaders, and submit to them...as those who will give an account."

Josh took care that his attitude was not like it was when he came to Arrowhead to help in the summer crisis. He knew a handful of Crusade leaders could be wrong and perhaps out of God's will, that he was being "exiled" to

CHAPTER
TWELVE

South America to get him out of their hair. Yet, he trusted in God's sovereignty; all was in His hands ultimately.

As planning would have it, a Latin American Crusade in Mexico City had already been scheduled before Josh's new assignment. It was here that his heart was prepared for a ministry to follow.

Josh took several students as part of his crusade team. They toured Mexico and Guatemala for a number of weeks, beginning in the jungles before coming to the cities. A week before the meetings, Josh flew down to the Yucatan Peninsula to speak at a youth convention. Tropical rains pounded the jungle town and Josh contracted malaria.

On the way back to the airport, the Jeep taking Josh got stuck in mud. Though feverish with a temperature of 104°, Josh got out and helped push and pull the Jeep out. By the time he got on the plane and landed in Mexico City, he was too sick to transfer from the hotel (where the students took him) to the local hospital.

The fever would not subside and Josh began to dehydrate. A nurse came to the hotel, but spoke no English. Josh spoke Spanish, however, and when he was strong enough to talk, was able to get water or medicine when he asked.

Students Barry Leventhal, captain of the UCLA football team, and Nancy Freedman, first runner-up in the Miss California contest, were in the city to give their testimony. Josh was to speak. Other students came to share their testimony, too. One of them was Leslie Simpson, Paula's twin sister.

Josh was like a brother to her, and when she saw how sick he was, she called home to ask for advice. Josh got on the line to talk to Vivian Simpson.

"Josh," she cried, "is that you? You sound awful. Isn't there a doctor there? What are you doing for your fever?"

"Leslie...and nurse...cold towels...helps," he said weakly.

"Oh, Josh," Vivian cried, "I feel so helpless. What can we do?"

JOSH

"Pray...." he said simply.

Leslie kept applying the cool, wet towels to Josh's face, arms and chest. The fever didn't leave, but it didn't get worse either.

A doctor finally came and determined Josh had typhoid as well as malaria. In four days he had dropped nearly 25 pounds.

Ten nights of crusade meetings were planned, with thousands of dollars spent on the arrangements. Something had to be done. The doctor gave Josh massive injections of antibiotics and vitamins.

The medication enabled Josh to be driven to the meeting each night, deliver his message, and return to the hotel.

The crowds were unusually large. Thousands had come out to hear the American and he did not disappoint them. The American athletes and beauties contributed their part, too, and a number of people were dramatically converted.

After the invitation one evening, one young Mexican, carrying something, all but ran to the front from one of the distant rear seats. Josh saw that he was carrying a huge shoeshine case. It was obviously important to him, his business. The case was beautiful, inset with expensive stones and trimmed with intricate carvings. The man placed the case on the altar, signifying he was giving everything to Christ as he dropped to his knees in prayer.

Josh and the other Americans were visibly moved by the gesture. Josh recalled he had once placed his law books and career on the altar, but not himself. In a quiet moment of consecration, Josh now gave himself to God.

The routine was the same for the ten nights of the crusade. Finally, on the last night, Josh spoke on the life of Daniel. The message ended, and as he gave the invitation, Josh collapsed into a chair on the platform. A doctor came to him and gave him a massive dose of Vitamin B_{12} and adrenalin to give his heart additional momentum, then ordered Josh back to his hotel room.

He was lying on the sofa the next day, feeling a bit stronger, and making plans to go home. The telephone rang and Leslie reached for it. "I'll answer it for you." She picked up the receiver, "Hello...."

CHAPTER
TWELVE

"Uh...oh, I'm sorry—I asked for Mr. McDowell's room," a man's voice said.

"This is Mr. McDowell's room. Who is calling, please?"

"This is Bill Bright—who are you?"

"I'm Leslie, Dr. Bright. Just a minute—Josh is in bed, I'll carry the phone to him."

Josh groaned. He could imagine what Bill Bright must be thinking. Leslie, in her innocent naivete, would not have any idea that her conversation must have sounded quite compromising. He quickly explained to his superior about his illness and how a few of the students had taken turns caring for him when he was so sick.

Bill Bright hadn't called to question their propriety. He wanted to know how the meetings were going and how the follow-up was being handled. He hadn't realized Josh was sick. Satisfied now that all was being done well, he told Josh to come home where he could get better care and rest.

◇———◇———◇

By late summer, after Josh's assignment to Argentina, he began to prepare to leave.

There was one item of business he felt was still unfinished, however. He made an appointment to see Paula. It had been nearly six months since they broke off their relationship in San Diego.

He was stunned, at their meeting, when she told him, "Nothing's changed regarding our relationship, Josh. I'm engaged to someone else."

Josh's heart began to pound. He hadn't expected to hear that. She told him who it was. He was a mutual friend.

"It isn't really all that sudden," Paula explained. "He came to me after you and I broke up and told me that he's loved me more than a year, but never said anything because of you. He told me that he's been silently trusting God that he could marry me. He asked me to pray about it, and...well..."

Old feelings had not been fully dealt with. Josh still loved her, yet knew he could not hold on to her. His eyes moist, he blinked and said quietly, "I...I understand." Then he stood up to leave. "Well...if there's ever anything I can do for you...just name it. You'll always be very special to me.''

She smiled, her brown eyes radiant with appreciation.

Getting ready for his trip to South America was not easy. To ward off typhoid, malaria and other bugs, Josh got the usual complement of shots and renewed his passport.

He had already used up all his money. Fortunately, an old run-down hotel in Downey let him sleep there free while he tried to raise his support.

But all his financial contacts had been exhausted. He still lacked $375 in support. He added up all his checks to see if maybe he'd made a mistake in addition. He counted the money three times and the answer was always the same—$375 short.

Josh was scheduled to leave the next day. Yet, he couldn't leave without all his support money.

"Lord," he sighed, "I believe You want me to go. But maybe You don't. Maybe You're still not satisfied with my attitude about going. I really *am* willing to go. But You'll have to help. I've run out of ideas.''

That night, just before he retired, he heard a knock at his door. It was a friend from a church in Compton.

"I've been looking all over for you. I tried to locate you through your home church, and finally somebody remembered you were staying here," he said.

He handed Josh an envelope. "This is from our Bible study group...for your South American trip.''

"Thanks very much," Josh said gratefully.

"Well, I'll be going. It's ten o'clock.''

"Wait," Josh said. "Stay while I count it. I want to see how much of an answer to prayer you've given me.''

"You don't have to count it," the man said. "There's $375 in the envelope.''

CHAPTER THIRTEEN

"THE FIRST THING YOU SHOULD KNOW ABOUT CHRISTIAN WORK IN SOUTH AMERICA," an American missionary said to Josh upon his arrival, "is that we don't do things the way they do them in the U.S."

"How do you reach people?" Josh inquired.

The man shrugged. "It's difficult. Most Latin students are anti-American."

"They are?" Josh asked. "I haven't sensed that."

"Take my word for it, they are."

"How do you make contact, then?"

The missionary took a small business card from his wallet. "I had these cards printed up with my address and phone number. If I run into someone who's interested in spiritual things, I give him my card."

Josh shuffled uncomfortably. "Uh...well, I've come to serve you and your work. But would it be all right if I tried to start a totally new work—maybe at LaPlata University?"

The man shrugged again. "Whatever you want."

The University of LaPlata in Buenos Aires had a student population of 28,000. By the best estimates, only a little more than a dozen were born-again Christians. These were the ones the Christian missionary groups concentrated on. Often they sponsored a Christian service or meeting in one of the Christian student union buildings paid for by missionary funds from the U.S. These meetings usually attracted as many as 30 people.

Josh decided that some kind of approach needed to be tried which would reach out to the masses at the university. He started a program to learn not just the language (which he spoke well) but the regional slang and dialect as well. These were areas that most foreigners ignored and their stiff use of the language usually betrayed it. Even Spanish words which were correct and appropriate in Mexico, stood out as incorrect if used in Argentina or Peru.

Josh told Latin Americans, "I want to go back to the United States a better person. I want to learn from you."

With such an attitude established, Josh found the students friendly, eager to cooperate—not at all anti-American. In fact, they welcomed conversations with someone from North America. They already knew how Peruvians thought, how Argentinians or Bolivians thought. But none of them really knew how an American thought, and they *wanted* to know.

The Christian workers or missionaries had avoided getting into dialogue with many of the students. A number of them were radical in their philosophies and the missionaries had already written them off.

Josh worked hard to meet them and get to speak to them. Several leaders of the engineering *pensión,* a building which housed a fraternity-type of organization, asked Josh to come and speak.

He was prompt on the day he had been invited to share ideas with some 75 engineering students. As he came into the big lounge where he was to speak, he saw that the walls were covered—like wallpaper—with photographed fold-outs and pictures of nude women apparently clipped from *Playboy* or other men's magazines. Josh was momentarily unnerved, but saw that it was as innocuous as wallpaper to the students. They seemed oblivious to it—so he tried to ignore it, too.

The talk proved to be so interesting to the Latin Americans that they kept asking questions and prolonging the dialogue. What had started out as an hour's sharing turned into a 13-hour marathon.

When it ended, a large number of students indicated a spiritual hunger and agreed to meet with Josh later at which time he would explain how to become a Christian.

Josh had to be careful. The government labeled any organized student group as *political.* That meant that meetings held without permission were forbidden. Christians and Marxists were in the same category—political groups—and

CHAPTER
THIRTEEN

such activities were not allowed officially.

Josh called the missionary to tell him about the success he was having.

"I've been invited to speak in 58 different *pensiónes,*" he told him excitedly. "They let me talk about Jesus and are really open to the gospel."

"I find that hard to believe," the man replied coolly. "I've been in South America nearly 15 years and I've never seen it. I don't believe it can happen."

"But it *is* happening. Come with me to a couple of these. You won't believe their openness to the things of God," Josh said.

"You're quite right. I *don't* believe it. It's impossible. If you want to waste your time, that's all right. But I won't waste mine."

"But come and hear for yourself," Josh argued. "Don't write it off without seeing for yourself."

"I think you're overstating the situation," the man responded.

"No...I'm not. Please—come with me."

The missionary never came. Nor did others whom Josh called to invite. They all dismissed his claims as impossible—that things "just aren't done that way" in South . America.

Speaking in the *pensiónes* and meeting people on campus encouraged Josh to rent a meeting room where he could speak to many more people. He correctly reasoned that in order for all 28,000 students to hear about Christ, he'd have to speak to audiences of hundreds, even thousands.

Since his Crusade work was not recognized by the authorities, he could not rent a room on campus. Finally, he located a room in the Salvation Army student union building and they agreed to rent it to Josh.

Josh and a handful of Christians went out at night and pasted up 800 posters telling about the meetings at which he would speak.

"Drop everything and run if you see police," a Latin Christian warned Josh. "As a foreigner your arrest could have more significance than ours."

JOSH

The posters did their work, however. They drew an audience on the first night of the meetings, and the crowds came in larger numbers on successive nights.

The Marxists, on the other hand, seldom had more than one meeting when a speaker came. They knew that the Communist speakers could not draw crowds which would come back after the first night.

Marxists were not his only adversaries. There were various other groups which opposed Christianity. One of them was a cult of spiritists whose religion was based on Satan worship and the occult. There were fascist organizations that were even more radical and militant than the Marxists.

Josh's genuine love for the people—Marxists, fascists, spiritists included—transcended their beliefs. He approached them always as persons and even they noticed his love for them.

"How can I have a love for all the people such as you have?" a Communist woman asked him.

"My love doesn't originate with me. It's supernatural," he told her, explaining the power and reality of God's love to her.

Some of those who opposed him mellowed, but some adversaries only became more aggressive. At one meeting where Josh sat across a table from a satanist, he was sharing his testimony with several dozen students. Under the table, out of sight, the satanist was kicking Josh's leg unmercifully to watch his reaction. Josh only smiled at him. After the message, Josh asked for questions. The satanist, by way of apology and admission, asked how he could follow Christ. "I believe now the Spirit of God is more powerful than the Spirit of darkness."

Some threats were more dangerous than this, however. Josh was to address a crowd from a free speech platform in the square. His subject was where the revolutionary Che Guevara failed. On the way to the square, Josh crossed the street and was about to step up on the curb. A ten-story building was under construction there. Two students ran to him, yelling for him to stop. Two other men pushed him off the sidewalk into the gutter. At first Josh was annoyed, then he saw they were trying to save his life. He looked up to where they pointed and saw several radical students on an exposed upper story level. They were poised

CHAPTER
THIRTEEN

with cement construction blocks to throw them down on Josh. If even one had hit him, he would have been killed.

Sometimes the rivalry between the groups had humorous overtones. If posters were put up around the university on Tuesday night for a Thursday meeting, by Wednesday night the Communists would paste their own poster over those promoting the Christian event. Then the Christians began ordering twice as many—pasting over the paste-overs still *later* Wednesday night.

Or, the Christians would change the size of their posters. It caused for a strange juxtaposition of messages. Readers thought "Professor McDowell...speaker..." was a Communist speaker talking about the invasion of Czechoslovakia, then in the news.

In one instance, Josh's posters were defaced with big red "CIA" painted over them. As it turned out, such efforts and defacing of the Christian posters only served to bring out bigger crowds.

Josh had also learned how to deal with hecklers. He'd arrive early before a speaking engagement and ask fellow students who the agitators were. They were usually there to disrupt the meetings. Josh sought them out and engaged them in conversation. In a few minutes of asking their names, interests and latest girl friend, Josh could use this information to advantage when the man later proved to be a professional agitator.

"Now, Ramon, you don't really mean that," he'd grin knowingly. "Didn't you tell me you were from Bolivia—how could you possibly know what the issues are here at LaPlata. Are you sure you aren't here just to check up on Maria?"

Josh was so disarming and friendly that the crowd often thought the agitator and Josh were friends. How could they take seriously the heckling of someone who was only a half hour earlier engaged in light conversation and laughter with the speaker?

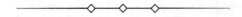

One Wednesday night Josh had finished a language class at the university and left for home. It was quite late as he approached his apartment. He unlocked the door and went inside to be met by four obviously agitated men. Josh's roommate, Miguel, introduced them as students.

Out loud he said to Josh, "These men have been waiting nearly four hours to see you. Can you talk to them?" Then he whispered as he walked by the door. "I don't know who they are—but I can *feel* their hatred in the room. Be careful."

"I will go for a walk so you may talk," Miguel said, anxious to get out.

Josh did not know them either. "Let's go across San Martin Plaza to the cafe for some coffee. We can talk there."

The men said nothing, but followed Josh. As they walked, Josh could sense the hatred in the air. At the coffee shop, Josh picked out a large table and sat down. The four others all sat down on the same side, opposite Josh.

"I don't believe we've met. Why don't you tell me who you are and why you wanted to see me?"

A tall blond man, not as muscular as the others, seemed to be their leader. Although he was more slightly built than the others, his look and attitude were no less menacing. He introduced himself as Steve. "We belong to a movement which the government has outlawed," he explained. Josh knew the organization to which Steve referred. It could best be characterized as fascist—with many similarities to the Nazi Party. In fact, some of their leaders idolized Hitler, Mussolini and other dictators. It was becoming one of the fastest-growing organizations in South America, despite the fact it was banned.

Steve and his associates began to talk to Josh about the organization's aims, goals and programs.

"We're here to recruit students to attend our national convention in Mendoza," Steve said.

"I see," Josh said. "Why are you telling me this?"

"Because," Steve replied, "we want you to join with us. To travel and lecture for us in the universities."

"You want me to do *what?*"

"Several of us have heard you speak. You are a convincing lecturer. You could help our cause tremendously."

"Gentlemen," Josh said shaking his head, "I'd be stupid to do that. Why should I give up a *great* cause to join a lesser one?" He went on to explain why he felt Christianity

CHAPTER
THIRTEEN

was so much better a cause. They talked for six hours. About three in the morning, Josh could see that Steve was still holding firm to his convictions, but that the other three were softening.

"I want you guys to know that God loves you and that I'm going to be praying for you," Josh concluded.

At that Steve jumped up. His chair clattered loudly to the floor. He knew he could not convert Josh to his cause. He screamed at Josh and threatened him, "You'd better not leave your apartment alone...or you're a dead man!"

Miguel was frightened for Josh when he heard what had happened. "I was afraid you were already dead when you did not come back," he said.

"Well, don't worry, Miguel," Josh reassured him. "God has everything in His hand. He has already seen to my safety. My schedule calls for me to leave for Bolivia today."

Before he left for Bolivia, Josh received a phone call from a missionary who had heard what had happened. "Be careful, Josh," he warned, "these guys mean business. These four are part of a group of ten who are the ones who bombed a convention site where several people were killed."

"Are you sure?"

"There's no proof, of course," the missionary said. "That's why the police can't touch them. But everyone knows they were the ones. Privately they boast about it."

"But I only saw four men" Josh said.

"Six of them came earlier to the university. They heard you speak on the significance of the deaths of Dr. King and Robert Kennedy. Four of these six came forward to receive Christ after the meeting," the missionary reported.

"I see."

"The other two sort of dropped out of sight. The four who didn't go with the first six were the ones who came to your apartment."

"No wonder their leader was upset," Josh smiled. "Four of their group are Christians—and three more thinking, if I read them right."

"Well, just be careful."

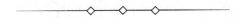

Josh had two weeks of meetings scheduled in

Bolivia. On the plane from Cochabamba to LaPaz, Josh sat next to a Roman Catholic nun. During the conversation, as usual, Josh steered the discussion to spiritual matters. He told about his life before and after his decision to receive Christ.

"I'd like to share a booklet with you," he told her. "This little booklet really helps me communicate my faith. You might find it helpful in your work."

As he opened the four laws booklet, the nun exclaimed, "I know that book. It is from God!" Excitedly she told Josh, "Four years ago I was in North America...in Toronto. I was walking down the street. A businessman greeted me when we both stopped for a traffic light. He asked me if I had ever heard of the 'Four Spiritual Laws'—just as you did. He asked me if I had a moment to listen as he shared. I listened for about 15 minutes and was greatly distressed. I saw for myself that although my life was given to the church, Jesus was not personal in my life. I prayed with that man a prayer to receive Christ. He gave me the booklet and went on his way."

"That's terrific," Josh smiled.

She nodded, adding, "I work on the other side of the Andes Mountains...in Bolivia. It is way back in the jungles among the Indians. I took this booklet and translated it into the many dialects of the Indians. Many are becoming Christians after we read it to them."

Josh settled back in his airplane seat, silently praising God. "Lord, some day I pray You'll let me meet the businessman who gave this little nun from Bolivia the Four Spiritual Laws booklet."

While in Santa Cruz, Bolivia, for meetings, Josh was suddenly afflicted with terrible pain. He woke up with an abscessed front tooth that grew increasingly painful. Even air going over the tooth caused him to all but scream out in pain.

He talked to several doctors and dentists. They all told him to have the tooth pulled. In this remote, semi-tropical country, however, Josh wasn't convinced that such an action was right. If, after pulling the tooth, the infection spread, he would be no better off than now.

Finally, Josh found a Jewish dentist in Santa Cruz

CHAPTER THIRTEEN

who told him, "That will be no problem. I will not need to pull it. It is an easy treatment."

Josh went to the man's office. He had a great deal of equipment, not as up-to-date as an American dentist's office, but adequate. The dentist started his drill and poised it over the abscessed tooth. The drill bit whined and dug into the enamel. A stream of pus and putrefaction shot out and the pain left immediately. The dentist filled the offending tooth and gave him a bill for $3.50 in U.S. money.

Josh later met an American student about his age in the post office in Santa Cruz. Josh went up and introduced himself, asking, "What do you do?"

"I go from country to country down here setting up cultural exchange programs," the young man replied, adding, "What do you do?"

"I travel and speak at colleges and universities," Josh said.

"What do you talk about?"

"Here—let me show you." He took out a four laws booklet.

The American swore and yelled, "Get that out of here! I'm not *interested.*"

"B-but...."

"Look, this salvation bit isn't for me, okay? Just leave me alone."

Josh apologized. "I'm sorry if I've said something to offend you."

"It's not just you," he told Josh. "I've been in Latin America two weeks. Thirteen days, actually. And in thirteen days, four different countries, I've had *ten* people approach me with those Four Spiritual Laws."

"Really?" Josh answered. He was impressed with Crusade's outreach and influence. He added, "Maybe God is trying to get you to listen."

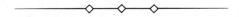

Before he left Bolivia, one of the missionaries who had arranged this tour, observed, "Josh...I've noticed something amazing. You speak in the usual broken Spanish of someone who has learned a language that isn't native to him."

"Doesn't everyone who comes down here?" Josh asked.

"Yes. That's not what is strange. You see, you speak in broken Spanish until someone asks you a tough question...the kind where a wrong phrase or word might confuse him. When that happens, your speech becomes a perfect Spanish. As if you were a native. Then, when you've answered the tough question, you revert back to the broken 'foreigner' style."

"That is strange," Josh concurred. "A missionary in Peru told me that same thing. And I discovered the same thing in Argentina. The only explanation I can give is that I prayed that God would give me boldness in speaking. I'm always relaxed then—and somehow God must give my brain a little nudge from time to time."

Josh returned to Argentina and his schedule of classes and meetings at the university. He heard someone call out his name on the way home from a meeting one night. He turned to see Steve, the leader of the fascist group at LaPlata.

He wondered if he should respond or find help, after the threat given just a few weeks ago.

"Wait—it's all right," Steve called. He seemed much less intimidating by himself. As Steve got closer, Josh saw that he was no threat.

"What's happened to you?" Josh asked. Steve was a mess. His clothes were unkempt, as if he'd been sleeping in them. He was dirty—and looked almost like a fugitive. "What's wrong?" Josh asked again.

"I've had a...uh...personal crisis. I've been looking for you."

"Why? What do you want?"

"I think you're the only one who can help me."

Josh gestured across the plaza. "Let's go over to the cafe...."

"No!" Steve interjected. He seemed nervous. "I...I can't go there just now."

Josh shrugged. "All right—what about my apartment at seven tomorrow morning?"

"All right," Steve agreed.

"By the way," Josh wondered, "how are your

CHAPTER
THIRTEEN

friends doing?'' The question was asked as a friendly gesture. However, it seemed to strike Steve full in the face.

"They joined your party," Steve said disgustedly. "Seven of our ten best leaders have been lost to Christianity. It has completely wiped out our movement at LaPlata. And I feel responsible. I will be held accountable."

"Well, let's talk about it in the morning," said Josh. "I'll see you at my apartment at seven."

Steve never showed up for that appointment the next day. In fact, Josh never saw him again.

Two days later, a husky black man came up to Josh in a local print plant where Josh was having more posters printed.

The man asked point blank, "Did four men come to your apartment a few weeks ago?"

Josh was hesitant to respond. He was leery of CIA agents and their counterparts.

"Why?" he asked. "Who are you?"

"Two weeks ago, three of my associates quit our party and joined Christianity. I have talked with them and they've met with me. I see big changes in their lives. I want that for myself. How can I be a Christian?"

In Chile, Josh learned a principle which is called "the authority of the believer." It was a concept which grew out of an experience two years earlier during "Bal Week," the Easter evangelism meetings at Balboa Beach when the Crusade group was competing against the *Socrates Den* people.

During the André Kole meetings, one of the fraternity men was trying to disrupt the meetings.

He had a new "souped up" Dodge Dart, with racing equipment. The muffler was unusually noisy, too. The student would pull up in front of the place where the Crusade meetings were going on.

Sitting out front with the car in neutral, he'd race the engine. The sound was most disruptive. But for added measure he'd slam the car in first gear and snap the clutch. The Dart would squeal for more than half a block. Then he'd back up and repeat the sequence.

"If he does that once more," Josh said to Gene Huntsman, one of the Crusade staff members, "we'll lose our

134

crowd. The meeting will break up. There's a lot of tittering going on now.''

"Shall I call the police?" Gene asked.

"It'd take them too long to get here," Josh reminded him. "I think Satan is trying to break up this meeting. As believers, we have an authority over Satan's power.* Let's call on Christ to exercise that power and authority.''

Josh and Gene prayed, reminding God of the value of maintaining proper order so the hundreds of students inside would not be distracted from making a decision for Christ by the car. The driver pulled up again and started to race the engine again.

"Satan," Josh ordered, "in the name of the Lord Jesus Christ and through His shed blood on the cross, I acknowledge you are defeated. Cease your activities in this area.''

The driver let the clutch out and floored the accelerator as before. But this time, there was one single noise as the entire rear end of the Dart seemed to explode. Parts scattered all over the street and the engine died immediately. The car was totally disabled. Thus ending the distraction.

Coincidence? Josh knew better. He thought often of that experience, and in South America had many opportunities to put the principle to the test again.

Josh was quick to point out to his fellow believers, "We don't have *power* over Satan. We have *authority*...authority to invoke *God's* power.''

There were times Josh exercised this authority and witnessed remarkable, miraculous results.

One such occasion took place during a period of unrest in the late sixties. Nelson Rockefeller had been appointed by President Nixon to take a fact-finding mission to South America. Many Latin students protested the selection of Rockefeller saying that he had too many financial interests in South America to be objective in reporting to Nixon.

Radicals promised demonstrations, even violence, for Rockefeller.

*Luke 10:19

CHAPTER
THIRTEEN

Josh had planned an itinerary that coincided with Rockefeller's trip—but preceded him by a week. It was a tense situation. In Chile, Josh was met at the airport in an armored Jeep. The country was under declared martial law.

The Latin American director of Campus Crusade in Chile was even afraid to introduce Josh as an American. Since he had been Canadian director of Crusade and came to South America directly from Canada, that's how he introduced Josh—hoping the students would assume Josh was Canadian. But Josh did not want to appear ashamed to be an American. He told the students where he was to speak.

At first, Marxists threatened to burn down the university if Josh was allowed to speak. But Christian students persisted. They proved the Marxists were in the minority by getting a majority of students to sign a petition compelling the university to reconsider. Josh was allowed to speak in the student dining room. Although they didn't cancel his talk, Josh could sense real tension in the air when he came to speak.

Josh looked inside the building. All the lights were out except one bare bulb above where he was to speak. They had unscrewed all the other bulbs.

"I feel like Daniel going into the lion's den," Josh whispered to Miguel, who had accompanied him.

When he was introduced the Marxist leaders presented him with several large posters of Marx and Lenin. It was their way of mocking Christ. There were some 75-80 hostile students in the room. As he began to speak, they booed, hissed and started throwing things at him. He had tried to speak about the basic errors of the student revolutionary movement, but the crowd was so disruptive and hostile, Josh wondered how things would go if they deteriorated.

He stopped. Quickly he exercised the authority he had as a believer to demonstrate that God's power was greater than Satan's.

Josh began to speak again, but this time he began to tell how Jesus Christ had changed his life.

At the mention of Christ's name, there was sudden silence. It happened so quickly that it stunned Josh. He momentarily lost his train of thought. But then he resumed giving his testimony—and continued uninterrupted for 45 minutes.

Now the words were falling on interested ears as the Holy Spirit began to work among the group. By eleven o'clock, they adjourned to the kitchen for pie and coffee. The students' attitude had changed completely.* They asked questions—not about politics—but about Jesus Christ.

After nearly two years in Latin America, Josh McDowell was one of the most popular lecturers going from one university to another. He drew such large audiences that small dining rooms or student union halls were no longer adequate.

He lectured in rented auditoriums seating 2,000 people and often the planners had to turn people away.

His facility with the language was so well mastered that Josh was now *thinking* in Spanish, which gave him added ability in debates with Marxists or others.

Yet, not only had he developed into a popular international lecturer. He was seeing unusual spiritual results for his efforts. Students were becoming Christians by the hundreds, and the total more likely in the thousands.

The reputation of Campus Crusade for Christ in Latin America was not only favorable, it was outstanding.

Reports of Josh's ministry were noted by Bill Bright, who called one of his top assistants in.

When Dr. Bright learned what had really happened and how Josh was "exiled" to South America, he said, "It's just like the story of Joseph in the Old Testament—'man meant it for evil, but God turned it to good.'

"I want you to call Josh McDowell back to the States," he continued. "I believe the time is right for a work like the one he's doing in South America to be done right

---

*Josh was to learn later that some of this group had planned to disrupt the meeting then leave for a meeting of other radicals planning violence to the American motorcade into the city. The students did not leave. The violence never materialized, either—Rockefeller's visit to this country was cancelled.

CHAPTER
THIRTEEN

here. Get him back here as soon as it's convenient for him to come."

The handful of leaders who would have harmed Crusade because of their strange beliefs or their selfishness were now gone. New leadership had emerged from among the ranks of Crusade field workers, experienced, Spirit-filled men dedicated to the original purposes and goals of Crusade and Bill Bright. And the experiences Josh had encountered in Latin America merely equipped him for greater things for God.

When "Swede" Anderson called Josh in Argentina to tell him to come home, he explained that Josh's faithfulness and submission to leadership were being recognized.

"The people who sent you there are gone," Swede explained. "Among them were some long-time associates of Bill Bright. Bill trusted them...and he got burned."

"And you're calling me back to the States?" Josh asked.

"Yes. We want you to come home and begin to do here what you've done down there."

"But, Swede," Josh said—wondering about those people whom Bill Bright trusted—"does Bill know he can trust me? Do you think he'll be worried that *I* might let him down, too?"

"Dr. Bright is the one who told me to call you. He's aware of the situation now, and *he* wants you back."

Before he returned to the United States, Josh had gone to Mexico to study communism and its methods. The training center was where Fidel Castro and Che Guevara stayed. It was where individuals were trained to be sent into other countries to promote revolution and disrupt the church.

Josh wanted to go there and learn the methods of the Communists so that he might be better equipped to debate Marxism or confront their atheistic principles with the gospel of Jesus Christ.

He discovered that the Communists were recruiting French-speaking priests and nuns from Quebec and other places and training them in revolutionary Marxism. Then they

JOSH

placed them in churches throughout Latin America where they could promote communism.

He had time to study and observe, but Josh could never remain silent about his faith. His Christian witness naturally led to problems at the school. Josh had led several priests and a nun to a personal relationship with Jesus Christ, and in doing so, exposed his true purposes. He was immediately expelled from the training center. Certain radical leaders, learning about his Christianity, came to threaten him.

"Well," Josh told them, "I'm leaving. You'll be glad to hear that I've been expelled. I'm going back to the United States."

One of the radical leaders pushed up close and glared. "You won't leave Mexico alive," he snarled.

Josh wasted no time in packing his belongings into his van and leaving the school.

He was driving down a blacktop road and approached a small rise. As he came to the top of the hill, Josh saw a car on the road ahead, stopped as a roadblock. *It has to be the radicals,* he thought.

The van was going just over 50 mph when he saw the car. He braked, swerved and tried to drive around them. They had been waiting for him—but not in a way he thought.

The radicals, clustered by their own car, suddenly took a teenaged girl they had picked up and literally threw her in front of Josh's van.

There was not time to stop or even react. He heard and felt the impact at the same time. His vehicle struck the girl's head and knocked her down. Then he heard the horrible sound of her body being wrapped around the wheel.

Josh screamed in horror and swerved to a stop in the ditch. His van bumped over the sharp lava rock, blowing out all four tires. Sobbing and terribly sick to his stomach, Josh tasted bile mixed with blood from a lip he split when the van went out of control.

The radicals immediately ran to their car, piled in, and screeched away at top speed. However, they left behind three "witnesses" who would swear that Josh hit the girl after driving recklessly.

Miraculously the girl was still alive. Josh called out in Spanish. "Get help! She must go to a hospital at once!" No one went for help. Equally providential was the fact that a

CHAPTER
THIRTEEN

motorcycle policeman came on the scene as soon as the speeding car disappeared over the hill.

He radioed for medical help, which came after what seemed to Josh to be an eternity.

Josh explained what happened and the "witnesses" gave their version. The policeman seemed to sense something wrong with the latter version. But although the policeman saw through their story, he had to arrest Josh, since he could furnish no witnesses of his own.

"Our law is different from yours, Señor," he told Josh. "I'm afraid the law concludes you are guilty until your innocence can be established."

Josh was taken to jail. It was a terribly dirty and primitive place, disease-infested and smelly. Before they locked him in a cell, they allowed him to make a phone call. He called his insurance company. He talked for some time, but finally got them to agree to fly in medical specialists to treat the girl's injuries and save her life.

When the Mexican agent for the insurance company finally came to care for the paper work, he wouldn't begin without getting what he called a "service fee."

"It sounds like a bribe to me," Josh muttered.

"Oh, no, Señor. It is just the way business is conducted in our country. My fee is $50 in American money."

Fortunately, Josh had taken his savings from two years in Latin America—some $1200—and converted it to traveler's checks before he left the university. He gave the insurance man $50 and got things started with him.

"I'll need a good attorney," Josh said.

"None is in our town," the jail guard told him.

"Then let me call the American consulate," Josh asked.

"Maybe tomorrow," the guard said, locking the huge barred door. It shut with such an awesome, ominous finality it made Josh's heart skip.

The cell was small, filled with many different kinds of insect vermin. At night the cockroaches kept him awake with their noisy scurrying.

In the daytime, it was too hot to sleep. The dank smells from the latrine hung in the air. The jail food was awful, though Josh tried to eat it. It gave him diarrhea and made him terribly sick.

In order to get food and drink his body could handle, Josh had to pay the guard a "service fee" of ten dollars to go across the street to get some bread and a bottle of warm Coke. If he wanted to eat three times a day, it cost him $30—ten dollars a trip.

They let him keep his Bible, so he waited the first week more or less patiently, as long as he could read God's promises.

He was moved by the horrible brutality of the place. Probably because he was an American, his jailers did not beat him. But when locals were arrested and brought in, they were taken to a room not too far from his cell. He could hear their screams as the guards beat and tortured them unmercifully.

During the first part of his second week in jail, he began to read Paul's prison epistles and took a strange new comfort in them and appreciation for the apostle's prison experiences.

Josh asked for a pencil and drew prophetic charts on the dingy stone wall of his cell. He also drew diagrams for the four laws and detailed explanations of them in Spanish.

One of the guards seemed interested in the charts. When told it was the plan for Christ's second coming, he was even more interested. He was joined by two others when Josh began to tell them about it.

By the end of the second week, Josh had witnessed to 15 policemen or guards.

The motorcycle policeman who brought Josh in came to see him. "I know what happened," he confided to Josh. Perhaps he had even seen it. "But I cannot become a witness, or they will lock me up with you until you are tried."

"How long before my trial?" Josh asked.

The policeman shrugged. "Long time. Sometimes a year...maybe longer."

Josh groaned. "There has to be a better way for me to prove I'm innocent."

"Perhaps," the policeman mused. "I will go to the judge privately and see...." Of course, it would require a $50 "service fee."

CHAPTER
THIRTEEN

Knowing the language made it bearable. For someone who didn't understand Spanish, or the local dialect, it would have been even more grim than it was for Josh.

The judge and policeman worked out a plan whereby character witnesses could testify on Josh's behalf. It could be arranged by telephone for "service" fees and—now a new one—"legal" fees. The "legal" costs took all but $400 of the money he had left, but he was released two days later.

Josh went to the garage to claim his van. It was parked in a cluttered back yard. The tires were flat and by now everything stripped from it. The radio, floor mats, mirrors, hub caps—everything. Even his belongings—clothes, files, books, even his notes—were stolen.

The garage owner still had the gall to ask $200 for "repairs and storage" before he'd release the keys to Josh. Four cheap tires mounted on the van took all but $70 of his money. It was about how much he'd need for gas to get him to Arizona, still some 28 hours away.

Josh climbed into the van and headed for the Arizona border. He didn't stop until he reached Nogales and a phone inside an American gas station.

A Christian businessman from Phoenix gave him enough money for van repairs and expenses back home.

CHAPTER FOURTEEN

JOSH MCDOWELL HAD LIVED IN SOUTH AMERICA during one of the most violent two-year periods of U.S. history. The world looked on as not only America, but the entire planet, seemed bent on destruction:

January, 1967	—Three Apollo astronauts burned to death in a spacecraft fire.
June, 1967	—Israeli-Arab Six-Day War. —Red China exploded its first H-bomb.
July, 1967	—Racial violence exploded in Detroit, Harlem, Brimingham and other cities.
January, 1968	—North Korea seized the *Pueblo*. —U.S. had over a half-million men in Viet Nam. "Tet Offensive" in Jan-Feb. inflicted worst casualties.
April, 1968	—Martin Luther King shot and killed.
June, 1968	—Robert Kennedy shot and killed.
August, 1968	—Czechoslovakia invaded by Russia.
December, 1968	—Death toll from Biafra civil war and famine at one million.

JOSH

Throughout this brief period America's university campuses were breeding discontent which was to be born later. Free speech platforms promoted anti-draft and anti-war movements which often erupted into riots and violence.

In Latin America, Josh had watched these events unfold. These usually gave him an opportunity to speak. His messages, however, were not political in nature. He explored the quality of human character which *allows* the violence of war, racism, famine or suffering. By showing assassinations, riots and war in the context of the book of Romans and Law 2 (man is sinful and separated from God) of the Four Spiritual Laws, Josh was able to have an effective ministry.

To a certain degree Marxists in Latin America tried to lay the blame for America's "sins" on him, since he was an American and an easy target. But Josh showed that Communist excursions in Viet Nam, the Russian invasion of Czechoslovakia, and other such events denied their "purity" also.

"Don't give me your rhetoric and revolutionary slogans!" Josh would challenge in debates. "Tell me how you're going to change the hearts of people. Are you going to do it with bombs and burning down the university? I submit to you that you'll never change the world until you change the basic nature of man."

"You guys don't have the answers," he would taunt the radicals. "If you did, people would come to hear you. You guys come to a campus and get 3,000 to come out. But you wouldn't *dare* have a second night's meeting because no one would come! Yet, why is it our crowds grow *larger* night by night?"

The debates, where Josh was not only forced to think on his feet—but to do so in a foreign language—had been good training for him.

The Latin revolutionary fervor was now beginning to sweep American campuses. But Josh had been prepared for it, intellectually and spiritually. Compared to Latin America, speaking across the United States would be "a piece of cake" for Josh.

Typical American college and university students were idealistic on one hand and devoid of values on the other. They fought to the point of violence on the "immorality of Viet Nam" and racism. Yet, many of them undermined

CHAPTER
FOURTEEN

credibility in their moral standards by tossing away traditional values. Sexual promiscuity, drug experimentation, X-rated film festivals and anti-Christian lectures became part of the university lifestyle. Many of these were even funded by government or university grants and fees.

Josh met with Bill Bright and shared some of his experiences with Crusade's president. Josh knew Dr. Bright must still be smarting from the hurts caused by those who had left Crusade. He had trusted them. Josh wondered if, thus "burned," Dr. Bright would impose a list of restrictions on Josh's ministry.

The subject did not even come up. Instead, Dr. Bright reassured Josh of his trust and confidence. "A man who has truly learned the servant's role," Dr. Bright told him, "will never have difficulties with submission. Even when his leaders go wrong, he won't worry because he knows that God protects His own glory."

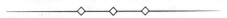

Josh was asked to speak at the Arrowhead Springs summer staff training session before he began his work as university lecturer.

He shared with the new Crusade staff people from his experiences. He told them about his own call to ministry with Crusade, even admitting his attitude problems when coming to take charge of the hotel administration several years earlier.

Josh also shared other spiritual concepts, refined "under fire" in Argentina. The messages in particular seemed to have an impact. One was based on what he had learned about the authority of the believer. The other dealt with honesty in prayer. He used the verse in Philippians 4:6 as his text: "Be anxious for nothing, but in everything by prayer and supplication with thanksgiving let your requests be made known to God."

"I used to feel guilty praying for something that didn't seem significant," he told them. "But the Bible tells me: First, I shouldn't worry about anything; second, I should pray about everything. Everything? Yes, everything—honestly. Let Him know exactly how you feel, how badly you want something. It'll do remarkable things for your prayer life, and your attitude."

JOSH

Most of the students were there at great personal sacrifice. They had scraped together their own money—what little they had—and could certainly identify with the needs Josh described.

About two weeks into the program someone told Josh that George, a student from Seattle, was dropping out and heading back home. But he hadn't said anything about it—he planned to just leave for Seattle quietly, which made Josh suspect something was wrong.

"What's the situation?" Josh asked George.

"Well, my father called. He got me this job with a construction firm. He says I can go to work and in two months earn enough for school this next year."

"Well, that's great, George," Josh said. "Is there another reason why you're leaving?"

"Yeah," George said brightly. "You know, I'll get in lots of overtime—and if I work a bit longer I'll not only have enough money for school, but for a Mustang."

"A Mustang?"

"Yeah...I've got my heart on a canary yellow Mustang...five-speed transmission, wire wheels," George told Josh excitedly.

"George," Josh said, "that's really exciting. But have you prayed about it?"

"About a Mustang?"

"Sure. You should be honest with God—even about Mustangs. Look, do me a favor. Before you leave for home, open your heart to God. Tell Him honestly how you want that car. Tell Him you deserve it. Be specific—pray that He'll help you get the yellow Mustang with the five-speed transmission and wire wheels."

At dinner, Josh saw George, still there. He saw him the next day, too. It was obvious George had either postponed or canceled his trip.

"Oh, I canceled it," he told Josh in response to the question. "I did what you said," George grinned, "and a funny thing happened."

"What was that?"

"Well, I told God how I wanted that Mustang...how I deserved it, y' know? But all of a sudden, God showed me why He called me *here*. He reminded me

CHAPTER
FOURTEEN

about Christ's death...and the Great Commission and all. When I saw the car in that light, well, I couldn't care less about the Mustang.''

In a similar instance, Josh talked with an athlete from the East Coast who confessed, "Josh, I'd like your advice. There's something in my life that interferes with my relationship with God. It seems I never want to read the Bible, share Christ with people—even be around Christians.''

"Well, what is it that interferes with your spiritual life?'' Josh asked.

The young man replied sheepishly, "Soccer.''

"Soccer?''

"Yes—that's all I think about, Josh. Soccer is the only thing that motivates me. All I can think about is being the best soccer player in America.''

"I see....''

"I want to be recognized when I go into a restaurant. I want to earn a lot of money. I think about this so often, I can't even pray.''

Josh referred him to the verse in Philippians 4. "Look," he said, "translate the verse this way: 'Be honest with God. Be anxious for nothing, even in soccer—by prayer and supplication with thanksgiving.' ''

The athlete wondered if Josh was being facetious.

"No," Josh told him, "I just think you should get this out into the light with God. Tell Him how you can't live without being the best soccer player in the United States. Tell Him you have to score more goals than anyone else. Explain to God how you want recognition, fame and money.''

"I can't pray that way," he said to Josh.

"Philippians says to pray in *everything*. Will you pray about it?''

"Okay...I guess so.''

Three months later Josh received a letter from him. "I appreciate your taking the time to share your thoughts with me," he wrote. "Boy, did God teach me a lesson! I did what you told me—I got the matter out into the light, being 'honest with God' as you said. When I told Him I had to be the best player in America and all that went with it, He just took that desire away. But a funny thing happened. In place of that desire, He gave me a new desire. Instead of being the best soccer player in America, I want to be the best in the *world*. I don't want to be recognized in a restaurant, I want to be so good I get invited to the White House.''

As he read the letter Josh began to feel as if he'd really "blown it" with the young man. But as he read through to the end of the letter, he was reassured.

"As I got the matter out into the light, over prayer,'' the man wrote, "instead of taking my desire away, God intensified it with a great desire. But God also changed my *motivation*. I don't want to be the best soccer player any more just to glorify myself. Now I want to do it to glorify Jesus Christ and use my experience as a platform to witness to people and in ways I never could imagine before.''

Josh noted God doesn't always work the same way with everyone. "The important thing,'' he wrote back to the soccer player, "is that whatever we do, we glorify the Lord Jesus, and trust God to give us the right motivation when we honestly get things out into His light.''

Paul Lewis was now directing a Campus Crusade for Christ work at San Diego State University. He also was now engaged to Leslie Simpson, Paula's twin sister. He and Josh had become friends when Josh was dating Paula two years earlier, and they had remained friends after Josh and Paula broke up.

Paul set up one of the first "free speech" debates for Josh following his return from Latin America. A pro-Marxist speaker had been scheduled by the University of California in San Diego who accepted the challenge to debate Josh.

All the groundwork and logistics had been done for the debate when it suddenly occurred to Josh that all his notes on the subject were in Spanish. This debate would be in English, obviously, so there was a mad scramble as Paul went searching for someone to translate Josh's Spanish notes into English. The notes consisted mostly of quotations and Josh wanted to be certain he quoted them accurately.

All went well. The debate drew a large crowd at the UCSD campus on the bluff in La Jolla overlooking the

CHAPTER
FOURTEEN

Pacific. Using the same tactics and intellectual strategies he had learned and mastered in South America, Josh was quite convincing to a number of people in the audience. Follow-up of those who showed an interest was quite productive for the Crusade staff. And, as a result of the positive results of the debate, the small corps of Christians on campus became boldly enthusiastic for Christ.

Josh was charged up emotionally, spiritually and intellectually to take on even more radicals in debates on other campuses. He felt much more confident as the result of a new revolutionary spiritual concept he had recently learned.

A Crusade speaker at the summer sessions had called Josh out of the audience to prove a point of the message. "Look at Second Corinthians 13:5," the speaker said. "It says, 'Test yourselves...examine yourselves! Or do you not recognize this about yourselves, that Jesus Christ is in you—'"

Josh was to respond to the questions which followed.

"Where is the King of kings?"

"In *me,*" Josh answered.

"Where is the mighty God?"

"In me."

"Where is the all-powerful God and ruler of the entire universe?"

"In me." As Josh (and those listening to the speaker) reflected, "I have total power—I have everything I'll ever need, because I have 'Christ in me'."

This boldness and confidence sustained Josh as he went across the country to different university campuses. In those first two years he would be on the road 26 out of every 30 days. He did not even have an apartment to come home to at holidays and didn't really take any vacations.

It was not long before Josh had developed a manual of policies and procedures to handle the logistics of speaking on a university campus.

The schedule was blocked out a year in advance. Josh would evaluate the Crusade work on a given campus and determine if they were organized well enough to administer the event.

"I have the 'easy' part," he told the campus directors. "I just come to your campus, speak, then move on. *You* have the hard job. Students will have to coordinate and run the entire operation. Committees will have to be selected six months in advance for the publicity strategy, finances, get your materials and posters printed. Then, after I speak, the real work begins."

Josh insisted that all students who marked a 3 x 5 inquiry card be followed up within 12 hours. That meant the student committees were often busy until two or three in the morning following a Josh McDowell lecture series addressing the letter or card to be mailed out before they leave.

The system worked well, however. With experience, Josh refined the system until each administrative function could be programmed precisely, freeing the staff for the one-to-one encounters as part of the follow-up.

There were a few who criticized such packaging as "too slick," apparently preferring a more serendipity approach to evangelism.

"The only reason I'm so firm about doing it this way is because it's done in an organized, orderly manner. God blesses it and we always see spiritual results. And there's still plenty of room for the creativity of the Holy Spirit to work," Josh said.

One thing did bother Josh, however. He wondered about the constant promotion of his name. The publicity for his speaking engagements, debates and meetings promoted him very visibly—"Josh is coming," "Go hear Josh," and "Josh is here!" Posters with his picture were everywhere when he came on campus.

"Do you think people will mistake my motives and think I'm on a giant ego trip?" he asked his friend, Dick Day.

Dick, ever thoughtful before answering, said, "I think you'll find that people respond better to an invitation to go hear somebody instead of going to hear a talk on some subject. You're a person. The publicity is a good teaser, and God is using it to get people to come and hear you. As long as you know your own heart and the motives are to glorify Christ, let it go. Don't worry what people might think.

CHAPTER
FOURTEEN

Remember, God protects His own glory. When you leave a campus, in six months they won't remember your name. But if you do your job—they'll remember and know Jesus Christ.''

At Duke University, Sam—a young radical student—hated Christianity so much that he went to different Christian meetings only to mock and disrupt them. He went all over the campus and painted four-letter obscenities on Crusade posters. If ever a Christian were bold enough to speak up in class, Sam ruthlessly mocked and shouted him down.

Sam was one of the first to show up when Josh was scheduled to speak at Duke. He found a seat at the front of the 500-seat auditorium where he could shout down the speaker and be especially disruptive.

Josh, not knowing this, saw an empty seat next to Sam and sat there during the preliminaries. As the crowd sat down and the program began, everyone was conscious of the bank of fluorescent lights which provided the light for the auditorium. They were blinking on and off intermittently and were quite distracting.

Josh leaned over to Sam, apparently mistaking him for a student Christian leader. ''I think Satan is trying to destroy the effect of this meeting,'' Josh whispered. ''Let's pray and invoke the authority of the believer for those lights.'' Josh prayed briefly—the lights continued to blink. But as soon as Josh was introduced and began to speak, they stopped flickering. Nor did they start again until the moment he finished. Then they started again.

At the end of the meeting, Sam came up to Josh.
''Did you see those lights?'' he asked incredulously.
''Yes,'' Josh answered simply and smiled.

Sam went away shaking his head over what he had witnessed—and thinking about the message he had heard, in spite of his intentions.

Later Sam's roommate came in and found Sam reading the Bible.
''What are you doing?'' his roommate laughed.
''I'm reading the Bible. You know that I've been

against anything Christian. Well, I've just seen something I can't deal with. Jesus is real. I've seen His power...I can't deny it any more," Sam admitted.

Sam accepted Christ. Later he became an instructor at Crusade's "Institute of Biblical Studies."

On another campus a young woman came to Josh after he had spoken on the subject of the Bible's historical reliability.

"How can you believe such lies?" she asked.

"Lies? I don't believe lies."

"Yes, you do," she said, then suddenly began to cry.

Josh was beginning to feel uncomfortable at that point. "What's wrong?" he asked.

"I started out as a Christian, but I don't believe any more. It's all lies."

"Give me an example of those 'lies'," Josh asked.

"Well, Moses didn't cross the Red Sea like it says in the Old Testament. He crossed the 'Reed' Sea."

"Who told you that?" Josh wanted to know.

"My professor. He said it wasn't the Red Sea, but the Sea of Reeds with only five inches of water. Then a strong wind blew so the Israelites could walk across."

"Your professor believes that?" Josh asked.

"Yes."

"That's fantastic."

"Why?"

"You mean your professor actually believes the entire Egyptian army was drowned in five inches of water? That's fantastic."

Still another time, at Boise State University in Idaho, a young Christian coed asked Josh if he would help her.

"How can I help?" he wondered.

"As part of our speech course, we have to give several talks. My professor told us we could talk about anything, so my first speech was about Jesus. My professor didn't like that, so he announced that he didn't want anyone to talk on Jesus again. Well, my second speech was on the Bible. And he said, 'After this no more speeches on the Bible.'"

CHAPTER
FOURTEEN

Josh appreciated her boldness. "Where do I fit in?"

"My next speech assignment is an interview of someone from a minority group. I figured that Christians are a pretty small minority—at least on this campus. Could I interview you in class as a member of a minority group?"

Josh smiled, "I'm game if you are."

The next morning she conducted a 45-minute interview with Josh. He used the opportunity to share his Christian testimony and explain his interest in biblical apologetics. He even worked in a "plug" for his meetings at Boise State.

Because of his earlier reactions, both Josh and the student wondered how her professor would respond. At the end of the interview he stood and said, "I don't usually tell the class the grade I give to a student. In this I'm making an exception. I'm giving you an 'A' for your work," he told the girl. "In addition," he said, turning to the class, "I'm going to require students in all six of my speech classes to go hear Mr. McDowell on one of the three nights he'll be here. And I want you all to take notes and write a paper evaluating what he says. Listen to his speaking and evaluate it for a class project."

Josh often spoke in classes such as this. In Philosophy classes, he addressed the issue of existentialism and Christianity. In Economics classes, Josh lectured on Economics, Christianity and Marxism, and in Sociology classes he spoke of the social revolution and Christianity. In every instance he presented a well-documented and researched lecture giving a strong defense, or apologetic position, for Christianity.

He began to see the value of documenting the historical evidences for the Christian faith into some form that would be helpful to Christian students who wanted to present an intelligent witness in class.

Working with a team of eleven students from nine different universities, Josh began to document his resource material. Nearly 5,000 man-hours were invested in the project, which was to be published as a book by Campus Crusade's publishing division, Here's Life Publishers, *Evidence That Demands a Verdict.*

The demand for scholarly, intelligent, well-grounded answers for matters of faith was there. Soon the book was into a second printing. Then a third. Successive printings eventually pushed the number of copies in print to over a million. The book became a runaway best-seller.

However, consistent with Campus Crusade policy, Josh does not receive any royalties. These funds are utilized by Campus Crusade to further extend their gospel ministries.

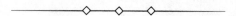

The itinerary for speaking was hectic to say the least. Being on the road all but four days a month required enormous stamina, dedication and will power.

But there was one advantage in not having a home to go to at the occasional breaks in his schedule.

It would have cost more—and taken two days just for travel—to fly from the East Coast to California. So, sometimes Josh would stay in the East to rest.

Once a year, he might fly to Bermuda or Jamaica for three or four days of rest, since it was closer (hence, cheaper to get to) than California.

He and another Crusade staffer flew to Montego Bay, Jamaica, for one of those four-day rest and relaxation stops.

The second day, Josh decided to drag Eddie out of bed and take the mountain railroad to Kingston, Jamaica, some 2½ hours away by train. He had heard about the ride from other tourists, as a beautiful side trip to take while on the island.

Neither Eddie nor Josh was enthusiastic about getting up before 6 a.m., but somehow they got to the train in time.

The trip through the jungle was magnificent. Josh was already glad they had gone when they were only 15 minutes into the scheduled journey.

From one of the other five railroad cars, Josh thought he heard music—hymns. Then he heard the unmistakable tune and words to "How Great Thou Art."

Josh was almost ready to go into the other car and meet the Christians who were singing when the music stopped. In another minute or two, a tall, good-looking black man entered their car. By his dialect they could tell the man was a native Jamaican. He was dressed in an old, but well-pressed

CHAPTER
FOURTEEN

shiny black suit. He was wearing a white shirt with a thin
black tie.

But his most outstanding feature was his radiant
face and wide smile. His presence filled the car and people
looked toward him, following his progress toward the front of
the car with their eyes.

He introduced himself and said, "Ladies and
gentlemen...I know you have a long trip ahead to Kingston. I
thought perhaps you'd like to sing a few songs with me." His
smile was widest now.

None of the passengers seemed to feel embarrassed
at the man's presumption. Josh just listened.

"I have some printed sheets with the words," the
Jamaican explained. "I'll hand them out. If you'll sing with
me, take one. If you'd rather not, just say 'no' and I'll know
you've turned it down in love."

Everyone took a copy and the man led them in the
singing of several hymns. He led them in singing "Amazing
Grace," "I Surrender All" and "How Great Thou Art."
Then he read some verses from the Bible, and explained them
briefly. Then, to the nearly 100 people in the train car, he
shared the gospel for about 10 minutes.

It was a clear, simple presentation of the gospel.
The man then gave the passengers an opportunity to pray to
receive Christ. And he moved on to the next car.

Josh was deeply moved by the man's devotion and
the simplicity with which he carried it out. He learned that the
Jamaican was a businessman. Five days a week, all year long,
he takes that train from Montego Bay to Kingston and back
again. In the round trip, he speaks to several hundred people
each day, presenting them with the truth and substance of
Christianity through faith in the Lord Jesus.

Josh felt a need to pray that he might demonstrate
through his life the compassion and commitment of that
faithful Jamaican.

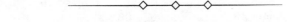

In 1970, Josh received the first of many threats on
his life in North America. A number of threats—some bluffs,
others quite real—had come his way in Latin America. But in
the States, he never thought they'd be a serious problem.

JOSH

Josh was on the campus of the school where he'd first been Canadian director of Crusade in Vancouver. It was here that an anonymous caller tracked him down.

"You won't live 30 minutes after getting to the Vancouver airport," the caller said, then hung up.

The call puzzled Josh. It had apparently been placed from New York City. How could anyone there know he'd be at this number?

Josh decided to give the matter to the Canadian authorities, who called both the Canadian Mounted Police and the F.B.I. in the States, since Josh was scheduled to fly to Austin, Texas, from Vancouver.

At the airport in Vancouver, the Mounties arrested several people who called themselves "Weathermen" who were waiting there for Josh.

Another person from the group was arrested in the Austin airport, waiting for Josh.

Two F.B.I. agents met Josh in Austin and told him of the arrest of Weathermen operatives.

"Just to play it safe," one of the agents said, "we're assigning two men to be with you around the clock while you're in Texas."

Dick Day was in Texas with Josh for this week. The two of them stayed in a student dorm. After the first meeting on the Austin campus, Dick and Josh went back to the dorm, to the room to which they had been assigned. It was reassuring to see, not only the two F.B.I. agents, but two burly football players—"bodyguards" assigned by the school. The "bodyguards" stayed in the room next to Josh and Dick, the federal agents in a room across the hall.

But about 2:30 a.m., one of the radicals sneaked past and quickly pushed open Josh's door and broke in. Before the man could do anything, however, he was instantly wrestled to the floor by the F.B.I. agents.

"Wait," Josh said, "don't take him away yet. I want to talk to him." After a few moments, things settled down so Josh could ask him some questions.

"Maybe you guys are out to get me because you don't really understand my message," Josh offered. "Let me tell you why I'm committed to Jesus Christ."

For 15 minutes Josh talked to the radical about a

CHAPTER
FOURTEEN

better revolution. The radical seemed to mellow after that. He even offered an apology of sorts, but warned, "You'd better be careful. The movement is out to get you and the others.* You're too vocal against communism and Marxism."

Like many radicals, this student took only one or two courses at the university. This was enough to qualify them as students, but in reality they were professional agitators.

Josh had met them at Western Washington State University, where he defused an angry mob ready to explode and march to the federal building to burn it down as a protest. He had met them at Berkeley, and at other campuses in California.

At Cal State, in Fullerton, California, Josh was speaking outdoors on campus when there was a sudden interruption. Police officers began streaming into the area and directed everyone away from the speaker's platform. As soon as they evacuated the area and escorted Josh to safety, a "bomb squad" went to a ditch behind the speaker's platform where Josh had been. They found 24 sticks of dynamite with a timer.

A policeman cautioned nervously, "If it goes off, it'll take the whole block!" But soon the bomb experts safely dismantled and removed it.

A similar thing happened at the University of Illinois Circle Campus in Chicago. In the midst of his speech on "The Errors of the Student Revolutionary Movement," Josh heard a girl scream, then a noise, followed by confusion. People were moved out of the area as police bomb experts were called in. Underneath the platform on which Josh had been standing was a container of explosives.

So Josh had to take threats on his life seriously, even though he expected God to protect him.

The Weathermen had boasted of their plans to burn down three buildings at the University of Texas and blow up their computer center.

The administration of the school approved the Crusade request for control of all the sound systems on campus the day Josh spoke. This would insure that, if the

*Referring to Crusade staff and students.

radicals disrupted the meetings, it would not be with the university PA systems.

The bodyguards accompanied Josh on campus. The F.B.I. agents checked for bombs around the platform and stayed with the football players near Josh on the speaker's platform, because of the threats on his life.

Thousands of people were there. Josh was completing his message when he spotted a group of radicals moving toward him, no doubt intent on taking over the microphones to incite the crowds into burning down the three administrative buildings.

Josh knew that if they took over the mikes it would be relatively easy for them to inflame the students to violence. He'd seen it happen many times before—in South America as well as the U.S.

Ad libbing the situation, Josh told the crowd over the public address system, "Let's pray." Instinctively thousands of heads bowed as Josh stalled for time. He suspected the radicals would at least wait until the prayer ended before taking over the mikes, so he prayed a lot longer than he usually prayed.

"We pray for Angela Davis...for Bobby Seales, for Chairman Mao...for Fidel Castro...for—" he named every revolutionary he could think of, beseeching God to show them the errors of their revolution, showing them how true social reform and revolution begins in a man's heart when he receives Jesus Christ.

At first, hearing Josh pray for the revolutionary "heroes" made the radicals hesitate. But when they heard the latter part of the prayer, they once again began to move toward the platform.

"—in Jesus' name, Amen," Josh concluded.

But as he uttered these words, a loud *"pfutt-too"* broke the air and the sound went dead. It sounded at first like a gun-shot. As Josh looked around, however, he saw that two radiator hoses had simultaneously blown out on the engine of the sound truck.

Without a sound system, the radicals could not organize the huge crowd of several thousand.

What happened next no one could have planned for—except the Holy Spirit. There were some 500 Christian

CHAPTER
FOURTEEN

students, trained as part of the "Operation Alternative" demonstration which brought Josh to the University of Texas campus. They were scattered all over the area, throughout the crowd.

Almost to a person, they began to share the four spiritual laws with small groups of eight or ten people.

There was even one Christian, paralyzed, and in a wheel chair. She had taken the four laws booklet and laminated it to a small wooden lap table. With obvious agony, she moved her arms to point to the diagrams, explaining the gospel to interested groups gathered around her.

The sight of her, with pain tearing at her arm every time she moved it, was one which many times lifted Josh. He'd remember her every time he'd be tired, sick or have a headache. That suffering would be minimal beside this example of courage.

A month after this incident, Josh returned to the University of Texas campus and spoke to the students. After a lecture, a student came up to Josh, unaware Josh was still wearing his lavalier microphone which picked up and amplified their conversation.

"The first time you were here, I came to throw things at you. The second time, I came to mock you. The third time, I came to listen," he admitted. "And five months ago, I gave my life to Jesus Christ."

The crowd heard this impromptu testimony and several more radical students began to curse and throw things toward the platform.

Josh learned that the object of their rage was formerly their leader. He was the most foul-mouthed, vocal and violent radical leader. He told Josh of sitting on the grass in front of the student union building after Josh's other message. After hearing Josh the second time, he was unable to sleep for a week. So disturbed and convicted by the third message, he sat in the grass as if paralyzed.

He told Josh, "I couldn't move. But I talked to God—I guess you'd call it praying—but I hadn't cleaned up my act yet. I said, 'God, I've never cared about You, never thought about Jesus Christ. But now my whole life is one big crock of.... If You're real, and if Jesus Christ is Your Son, like that McDowell says, then do something; show me.' That's what I said. Well, He showed me. I prayed that prayer you gave us to receive Jesus. I'm gonna trust Him to really change my life.''

Josh shook his hand and referred him to one of the Crusade students for follow-up counseling.

He had not noticed the student sitting in the grass in front of the student union—but he had taken notice of someone else.

There was a pretty woman in a bright dress at the back of the crowd. He had asked her if she was a Christian. When she said she was, he had asked her to come to the platform and give her testimony.

That was earlier. Now that the meeting was over and the follow-up in capable hands, Josh wanted to locate the woman in the bright dress and see if she'd have dinner with him.

CHAPTER FIFTEEN

DOROTHY YOUD HAD GRADUATED FROM NORTHERN ILLINOIS UNIVERSITY in May and joined the staff of Campus Crusade for Christ. After summer training at Arrowhead Springs, she was assigned to the campus of the University of Texas in Austin.

"Dottie" had not become a believer until her senior year in college. She had come from a very loving, church-going family who provided her with a comfortable, moral upbringing.

Dottie's dad was an insurance executive who was transferred often while she was growing up. However, instead of being afraid of each move, the family looked upon each one as an exciting new adventure.

Each time, one of the enjoyable family activities was looking for a new church at which they could worship. They visited various churches in every new city and discussed the values of each before deciding on the one they wanted to attend.

Dottie had grown up in Massachusetts. When she was in eighth grade, they moved to Georgia for a year. Then they lived in Connecticut, beside the Atlantic, for three years, before moving back to Massachusetts when Dottie was a high school senior.

In none of these cities, from New England to the Deep South, did they once find a church that presented the idea that Christianity was found in a personal relationship with Jesus Christ. Dottie was first presented with this concept at NIU.

She had gone to Northern Illinois University at DeKalb, Illinois—a college town about 40 miles west of

Chicago—to major in sociology with a minor in philosophy. NIU was a sentimental choice—she was the third generation woman in her family to go there.

By the time she entered her senior year, Dottie was pretty well convinced, through her Philosophy classes, that there was no God. Yet, that concept was in such sharp contrast to the beliefs of one of her friends, Dottie had not yet fully acquiesced to a world without a God.

Suzie, a young woman in Dottie's sorority, was "different" in the most positive sense. Dottie had chuckled when she had first met Suzie and felt how appropriately she had been named. Dottie, and nearly every other little girl, had shared childhood secrets with her dolls—there was always a doll named Suzie, with whom you could trust your innermost thoughts and secrets. Pert and bubbly, this Suzie was a living doll. She was a campus queen, representing their *Kappa Delta* sorority.

Despite the stereotype images, however, Suzie was more than a doll. She was an intelligent, personable individual who always seemed to have time to listen to the problems of others and somehow try to help them.

Dottie remembers that every time she had questions for her friend, Suzie responded first from her background of strong Christian convictions. Then she always went to her Bible for answers. This practical demonstration of faith at work outweighed the hours of academic doubt which had been directed her way in Philosophy class.

Dottie really liked Suzie, so when she asked Dottie to go with her on a fall retreat sponsored by a group called Campus Crusade for Christ, Dottie agreed. To be perfectly honest, however, it was the added selling point that there would be "a lot of great guys there" that won her over. That, plus the promise of a shopping trip into Chicago's loop.

The retreat was held in the northwest suburbs of Chicago in the spacious house of Harry and Gladys Dickelman, a Christian businessman and his wife who had opened their home to the collegians.

Dottie was captivated by the excitement of the Crusade leader who directed the meetings. She was also impressed with the caliber of the Christians who were there.

It was at this retreat that Dottie heard, for the first time in her life, the need for a personal relationship with

CHAPTER
FIFTEEN

Jesus Christ. She prayed to receive Christ and after that weekend, saw her entire life turned 180° as she saw God working in her life, giving her the qualities that she had so admired in the other Christians.

Following a full scholastic year of Bible study and growth through Crusade meetings on the NIU campus, Dottie was herself challenged to join the staff of Campus Crusade for Christ.

She paid her own expenses to Arrowhead Springs for special training and went home to raise support so she could work full time on a university campus for Crusade.

Dottie was assigned to the University of Texas and moved to Austin. There she lived in an apartment with three other single women, all Crusade staff members.

One evening the four of them were sitting around the table in the apartment following dinner. Over coffee, the conversation drifted—typically—to a discussion of the attributes and qualities in each of their Prince Charmings.

"I want a man who's intelligent and a football player," Helen dreamed.

"That's a contradiction of terms," teased Eileen.

"Yes," chimed in Nancy. "Besides football players get out of shape once they're out of school."

"Well, I still think an intelligent football player is what I want in a man," Helen pouted.

"Could it be because of that former fullback she dated last week?" Nancy wondered.

They all laughed as Helen blushed.

"You've been kind of quiet, Dottie," Eileen said. "What kind of man do you want to marry?"

"Me?" Dottie laughed, "Oh, I don't know. I guess someone bright, energetic, outgoing...probably someone interested in politics."

"Describe him," Nancy asked.

"Yeah...what's he look like?" Eileen wanted to know.

"Oh, blue eyes, I guess...dark tousled hair—"

"Hey," said Eileen. "You guys—you know who we should get Dottie together with?"

"Who?"

"Josh McDowell," Eileen smiled.

"Yeah!" the others chorused.

"Who's Josh McDowell?'' Dottie asked. "I've never heard of him.''

•   Dottie learned that Josh McDowell was the dynamic lecturer coming to the University of Texas campus. He had just returned from Latin America where he had debated revolutionaries and Marxists.

The Crusade director on campus had scheduled a whirlwind itinerary for Josh. In the mornings he spoke in classes. At noon, he usually addressed a local Rotary luncheon or leadership group. Afternoons he went back to classrooms or was interviewed by the press and by radio-TV people.

All this was before the primary purpose of his coming, the evening lectures.

If there were any "holes'' in the schedule, Josh would find a spot on campus for an outdoor rally or impromptu debate with the ever-present radicals.

Dottie attended Josh's first meetings. They were 40-minute lectures in various classrooms:

> "I appreciate the opportunity to visit a Sociology class today, because if there's one area today where I'm concerned as a Christian activist, it's in the area of the social problems we face....''

> "I always appreciate an opportunity to come into an Economics class, for to me, economics can be rather dynamic. That's why I majored in economic theory and why I address myself today to 'Economics, Christianity and Marxism.' ''

> "I appreciate the opportunity to share my thoughts with a Philosophy class because it's the one area where I think Christianity relates. I'll be brief, but I'd like to touch on the basic areas—the philosophical progression....''

Always his opening approach was the same, but Dottie was amazed that one man could know so much, be so able to adapt Christian truth to any specific course of study or academic discipline. She sat in as Josh spoke several times and said to Eileen, who was with her, "I wish I could travel all over and hear him. Every time he speaks I learn so much more. There's too much content to get in just one hearing."

"Yes," Eileen remarked, "I know what you mean." Then she added whimsically, "What do you think of him?"

Dottie thought for a moment, then said, "I want to marry a man just like him."

As part of the Crusade staff, Dottie was part of the team that accompanied Josh around the campus. She met him and had talked with him six or seven times, but Josh never noticed her. At a staff breakfast, he smiled and said, "I don't believe we've met—I'm Josh."

"Hi, I'm Dottie," she said, but was thinking, *we've met a half-dozen times. I wish you'd remember.*

"He doesn't even know I exist," she sighed to her friends later. "The first time we met, I sat across from him at the staff dinner, drinking in his every word. He evidently doesn't remember meeting me there. And another time, when he was lecturing on prophecy, he said, 'Uh, Sis...would you mind holding my notes while I talk since I don't have a lectern?' He thanked me when I gave him his notes at the end of the lecture—but he introduced himself *again*. He still doesn't remember meeting me. The same thing happened today—we've met six times and he still doesn't know I exist."

⋄ ⋄ ⋄

By the end of the school year, Dottie had also forgotten about Josh. However, she remembered him when, that summer, she went back to Arrowhead Springs and saw that Josh McDowell was to be one of the speakers.

His topic was "Love, Sex and Dating." He presented principles which were new to Dottie. She was extremely touched by his suggested spiritual principles of loving in a dating relationship. He gave her a great deal to consider.

During a time of reflection and commitment following his message, Dottie prayed, "Lord, these principles make so much sense to me. Thank You for sharing them with me through the message. Lord...these are the qualities I want in a husband...and I pray—even in this age of crazy values— You will give me a man who believes in these same things."

Dottie went up to the platform following the meeting to express her appreciation to the speaker.

"Hi, I'm Josh...I don't believe we've met," he said.

"My name's Dottie Youd," she replied simply.

"Where's your assignment?" he asked.

"University of Texas."

"Oh, yeah...I've been there before. Fantastic school. And a terrific Crusade work there."

"Uh...yes, it is," Dottie said.

"Well, it's good to meet you, Sis. I'll be back at Austin in the fall. Pray for those meetings," he said.

"I will," she promised.

At a free speech rally in September, Josh McDowell was addressing a crowd of a thousand students on the steps of the student union.

Dottie was all the way at the back of the crowd, sitting on the grass with her three friends. They listened attentively as Josh talked to the assembled students. Abruptly he stopped. Looking toward the back of the crowd, he said, "Excuse me...but you—" he pointed toward the four girls sitting in the grass—"the girl in the bright colored dress...are you a Christian?"

Dottie looked around her. She flushed to see that she was the only one in the immediate area wearing a dress of that description. She sheepishly nodded a response to his question.

"Would you mind coming up to the platform? I'd like to ask you to give your testimony."

As Josh continued his address, Dottie made her way to the platform. She was grateful that as a matter of training all Crusade staff people had been taught to give a concise, three-minute testimony of their faith in Christ. She had even helped train Christian students on campus to prepare that short a testimony. (It had been learned that because of the realities of "free speech" on campus, you could never count on keeping the microphone, so in three minutes you at least would get in the basics.)

CHAPTER
FIFTEEN

Dottie sat down on one of the folding chairs on the platform and waited for Josh to finish and call on her. As she sat there, she looked over the other Christian leaders on the platform. There were already several others there—more than enough for testimonies. *Why did he call me up?* she wondered.

There was a huge crowd there, but Dottie had given her testimony many times before at such events. She was not nervous, yet as she stood at Josh's request to give her testimony now, her mind went blank.

For several seconds Dottie stared numbly ahead. It seemed to her several minutes had gone by. Finally she spoke. Dottie spoke about Jesus Christ and what He had done in her life. It was longer than three minutes by the time she got her composure and shared about the reality of her faith.

When she concluded, she turned and went back to her seat on the platform.

"That was good, Sis," Josh grinned, "but it was *six and a half* minutes."

Dottie was immediately red-faced and apologetic.

When she sat down, the same question persisted. *Why did he call me up here?*

Josh did not introduce himself to her at the conclusion of the meeting. He was whisked away to another speaking engagement. Dottie's question was not answered because Josh left the next day for another university.

Several days later, the Crusade campus director at the University of Texas called Dottie in to his office.

"Yes, Walter?" she asked. "You wanted to see me?"

"Oh, it's nothing official. I just wondered about your long distance phone call...."

"Phone call?" Dottie asked. "What phone call?"

"Didn't you get a long distance phone call within the past day or two?"

Dottie tried to recall when she'd last called her parents—that was over a week ago. "No...I haven't gotten a long distance call—why?"

"Uh...well, never mind."

"Walter Steitz!" Dottie said in mock indignation. "You can't *do* that! You can't call me in here, get my curiosity up and then just say 'never mind.' What's going on here?"

Walter laughed and apologized, "I'm sorry, Dottie. I thought he would have called you by now."

"*Who?*"

"Josh...Josh McDowell. He asked me if you were dating someone. It seems he was going to ask you out for dinner before he left campus, but saw you talking with some guy. That's why he asked me if you were dating someone in particular."

"And...?" Dottie inquired.

"And I told him I didn't think you were. So he asked me if I thought you'd go out with him. I told him to call you. I gave him your number."

"Well," Dottie said breezily, "you'll be the first to know if he does." She left his office wondering if there was anything to the idea.

She waited for that phone call. Every time the telephone rang in the apartment, Dottie jumped. The call never came. She had never told anyone about the conversation in Walter's office, and by October, had dismissed the incident.

He probably had me mixed up with someone else, she reasoned.

Besides, just now her thoughts were with the plans for a Campus Crusade demonstration next week. Nearly 500 Christian students—some from other schools—were joining in a giant demonstration which they called "Operation Alternative." It would be to demonstrate that Christianity was a viable alternative to the radicals' cry, "Burn the campus down!"

Josh McDowell was coming back to spearhead the rallies and outdoor speeches. They even reserved all the sound systems to insure the radicals couldn't drown them out.

As preparations continued, Dottie was introduced to other Crusade personnel. She was having coffee with one young woman who confided a secret, "Guess who my roommate is dating," she gushed.

"I don't know, who?"

CHAPTER
FIFTEEN

"Josh McDowell," she answered excitedly.

"Really," Dottie replied, trying to even the inflection in her voice. "Is it serious?"

"I think *so,*" the woman replied. "He's called her three times in the past month."

Dottie's heart sank, but she said nothing.

Campus Crusade for Christ had organized the "Operation Alternative" for the University of Texas. Dick Day and Josh McDowell were helping to organize the rally. Josh flew into Austin from Vancouver and was given campus bodyguards after a threat on his life by the radical Weathermen organization.

Dottie's coffee friend rushed up to her during the preparations for "Operation Alternative."

"My roommate has a date with Josh McDowell tonight!" she said excitedly.

Oh, well... Dottie said to herself.

On Saturday, the demonstration was over. It was successful on several levels. Campus authorities were probably most grateful that it did, in fact, cool things off since Weathermen plans included burning down three administration buildings and destroying the computer center.

The Christians on campus, however, were pleased that so many of their brothers and sisters in Christ took a stand with them to make Christianity a vital issue on campus. Crusade's credibility as an organization had also been helped.

Dottie, in her "grubbies," was helping to dismantle the book table where the Christian literature had been offered. She was tired, but felt good at the results of "Operation Alternative." More students had showed up for their rallies than for the radical meetings. As she conversed with several other Crusade team members, Dottie was unaware of someone approaching.

"Hi, Dottie...."

She turned. It was Josh. "How did you know my name?" she asked.

He smiled. "Last month, at the rally in front of the student union. I'm Josh McDowell," he said. "We've met

JOSH

before—don't you remember?''

Dottie laughed in spite of herself. "Yes, I remember." She extended her hand.

"I've thought about you a lot since I was here last month," Josh told her.

"You have?"

"Uh-huh. And I was wondering," he asked shyly, "if you're free tonight...maybe we could go out?"

Dottie's heart began to pound. With tremendous effort she waited and replied in her most detached voice, "Why, yes...I suppose so," while her thoughts screamed *Yes! Yes! Yes!*

Josh smiled again, "Great. I'll pick you up at six. We'll have dinner, go see a movie, maybe have dessert later and—"

"But's it's almost four o'clock *now* and we're not finished with the clean-up!"

"Yeah—I figured you'd need a half hour or so to get ready when you finish here. See you at six."

A half hour, her mind echoed as he walked away.

Tired as Dottie was, she found a new reserve of energy to help her complete the clean-up details.

She raced back to her apartment and jumped into and out of the shower in record time. *A half-hour*—she'd need two hours and then some.

As she fixed her hair and dressed, Dottie began to get nervous. After waiting all this time for a call, let alone a date, she was scared. She only knew Josh through his platform personality.

Oh, no! she worried, *he'll want to know my thinking on the Arab-Israeli situation! He'll ask me questions about existentialism and Christianity...or my economic theories of Christianity versus Marxism or—*

"Help!" she prayed aloud. Then she reasoned, *I won't worry about my spiritual ignorance because I'm only a year-old Christian. I'll just listen and get to know him as a person.*

Josh put her at ease right away. He talked about his background and interests and asked about hers. He was genuinely interested and the two of them talked and laughed easily with one another. As they joked about their growing-up

CHAPTER
FIFTEEN

years and experiences, Dottie was glad he proved to be "a real person" and not just the super-spiritual platform person she had imagined him to be.

After dinner, they rushed to the showing of the movie, "It's A Mad, Mad, Mad, Mad World." It was an uproariously funny film which both enjoyed.

They stopped at a nearby coffee shop for dessert and coffee and chatted until the manager wanted to lock up and go home at midnight.

Their first day together was a great deal of fun and excited conversation. The next week, Josh—on his way from the West Coast to the East Coast—had the travel routed by way of Austin, Texas. The layover gave him several hours which he spent with Dottie.

The same thing happened when he traveled from East back West.

He also booked more meetings at the University of Texas.

Their dating was now a weekly activity. But their dates were also whirlwind events. Josh, by nature, is impulsive and energetic. He was ever eager to make the most of their time together, never content to do just one or two things. He crammed more fun and interests into a single day than Dottie imagined possible.

On a typical Saturday Josh picked her up for breakfast at a local coffee shop, from there they went to an art fair and browsed, looking at the aisles of paintings, sculptures and crafts several times before leaving. Josh brought two chicken dinners at "The Colonel's" and drove to the zoo park for lunch, where as soon as their meal was over, they walked through the cages and exhibits of the zoo, feeding the animals. Their evening was spent on a six-course Chinese dinner at a downtown restaurant, followed by a concert, play or movie. To conclude the day, they drove to some quaint place for coffee and dessert.

By the end of such a day, Dottie was absolutely exhausted. But she also noticed that they saw more of the city in two days together than she had seen in two years of living in Austin.

JOSH

In three weeks' time they had dated every weekend and Josh called her nearly every night when he was traveling. Despite the fact they had only had a half dozen dates by then, the couple sensed a growing seriousness of the relationship.

Josh and Dottie were invited to the home of a mutual friend for the Thanksgiving weekend. They spent even more time together, got to know each other better.

As their time together that weekend drew to an end, Josh took Dottie in his arms to say good-bye. He kissed her, long and tenderly, and slowly drew back.

"Good-bye," she said quietly.

"I love you," he whispered.

The words caught her by surprise. She had expected "good-bye" instead.

"I'm not asking you to say anything just yet," he whispered softly. "I just wanted you to know how I feel."

When he was gone, Dottie was confused, upset.

She felt she probably *did* love Josh, but wasn't certain of how serious his words were. After all, they had been dating only a month. How could he be so *certain?* That was what was so confusing—why she couldn't be certain that she loved him.

"Men are notorious for using that phrase lightly," a cynical friend had told Dottie. Was Josh like those who said "I love you" with the same sense of commitment as "Have a nice day"?

Dottie recalled a letter she had received from a friend who knew Josh and other women he had dated. "Have fun with Josh," the friend advised, "and enjoy your times together. He dates a lot of women, but he's honest. You'll always know where you stand—that the relationship is just for fun, a date crammed into his hectic schedule. He'll never lead a girl on. He'll never use the 'I love you' line because he respects you. If he ever does say it—he'll mean it."

The next time Josh visited, he began by kissing her and saying "I love you." He could sense her hesitancy in reacting to his words, so he elaborated. "I've only said that to one other woman," he explained. "That doesn't mean I'm expecting you to tell me you love me. I don't use the words 'I love you' unless I really mean it."

Dottie began to laugh.

CHAPTER
FIFTEEN

"What's so funny?"

"I'm sorry," she apologized. "It's just that I got a letter from a friend who warned me about dating you. She said you date a lot of women and have quite a reputation as a charmer. But she told me—almost word for word what you just said—'one thing you can always count on, Josh will never lead anyone on. If he says I love you, he means it.'"

Then the reality of it sunk in. She blushed deeply and felt her heart flutter when she looked into his eyes and saw his utter seriousness.

"I-I...give me time to think about it," she stammered.

In early December, Josh asked Dottie about her holiday plans.

"I'm going home for some meetings for raising my support in a couple of weeks. Then I plan to spend time with my folks—especially Christmas and New Year's at home. And you?"

"I'm going to Jamaica for a week to rest. Then after Christmas I have a lecture series that runs through New Year's."

"Are you free for Christmas?"

"Yes—a week before and the day after."

"Then come to Massachusetts," she begged. "There's no place on earth more beautiful at Christmas. Lots of cold and snow...we'll have loads of fun."

"All right," he smiled, "if you're sure it's all right with your folks."

"They'll love to have you. Dad's anxious to meet you. So is Mom."

◇——◇——◇

Josh was in Jamaica for a week for rest following a gruelling 90 days of 700 straight speaking engagements—nearly *eight* talks a day ranging from 30 minutes to three hours.

He was relaxing on the beach when he heard his name being paged on the hotel's public address system.

"Hello," he replied when the operator connected him.

"Josh?"

JOSH

"Dottie! It's great to hear your voice."

"Josh—I'm sorry to bother you, but I was wondering if you could do me a giant favor?"

"Anything. What is it?"

"I'm not doing very well in raising my support for next year. Is it possible for you to cut short your stay there and fly back early? I'd set up a meeting for you to speak and help me raise my support."

"Of course!" he replied without hesitation. "I'll leave tomorrow."

As he hung up the phone, he laughed. The hotel attendant took the phone and listened as Josh told him, "This *must* be love...for me to leave this tropical paradise and go back early to the snow and slush of Boston. But I can't wait to see her!"

As Josh's plane landed at Boston's Logan Airport, he looked out the window of the jet. His words were indeed prophetic. Snow was piled high in areas away from the traffic. The stewardess announced as they taxied to the terminal gate that the temperature was 28.°

Dottie met him at the gate and took him to the Youd home in the suburbs.

For the next nine days, the routine was exciting and eventful. Josh helped Dottie with her support meeting and worked some on the manuscript of a book he was compiling. The two of them went Christmas shopping, were caught up in the holiday social events in church, and spent time alone before the fireplace. The days passed swiftly, and even Dottie's folks sensed the growing seriousness of their relationship.

On Christmas eve, Josh kissed her, once again telling her of his love for her.

"Please," Dottie whispered. She pulled away from him. "Josh...I...we..." she stammered, "our relationship is happening much too quickly. It's all too sudden...things are happening too fast for me. I...I need more time...more room to think and pray about us. Please...let's...let's back away a little...."

Oh-oh, Josh thought, *I've blown it by coming on too strong.* "I'm sorry if I've pressured you," Josh told her.

Dottie knew that Josh had not backed off at all from using the expression, "I love you." Rather, if anything,

CHAPTER
FIFTEEN

he used it more frequently than ever. Now she knew for a fact where he stood.

Yet, she also knew that if she told him, "I love you" that he would certainly propose. Emotionally, she wasn't quite ready for that. *We don't know each other well enough yet—it's too soon,* she argued with herself.

"Listen," he told her, "I have to leave for Dallas tomorrow. I'll be there until after New Year's with the holiday conference. You'll have time to be alone, to pray. I won't bother you, or call you. I'll give you room to think."

"Thank you for understanding," she said, kissing him lightly.

Dottie flew back to Austin after the holidays and went back to her Crusade assignments. She had given the matter of their relationship considerable thought and prayer. She already knew she loved Josh. That wasn't the reason for her concern. She just wanted to make sure that if God directed, and the relationship developed, she would be able to handle it.

Josh called her that night.

"I'm on my way from Dallas to California for another speaking engagement," he said. "How was the rest of your Christmas vacation?"

She told him about all that happened since his departure on Christmas day. After several moments of small talk back and forth, there was a lull in the conversation.

"I love you, Josh," she told him.

"What was that?"

"I said, 'I love you'."

"That's what I thought I heard," he said brightly. "Hey!—how about if I fly into Austin next weekend?"

Her heart was racing now, but she answered, "Yes...next weekend will be fine."

Dottie lived that week nervously. Josh flew in from California and picked her up on Friday evening. They drove to a favorite restaurant beside the Colorado River in Austin and sat down inside by a window. The atmosphere was highly romantic.

JOSH

The waiter brought their salads then retreated. Josh held Dottie's hand, quietly said grace, shook out his napkin and put it in his lap.

She looked radiant and quite beautiful to him.

Dottie picked up her fork and dug lightly at her salad. "Tell me about your schedule for the coming year," she said.

"It's not finalized yet," Josh replied.

"When will you finalize it?"

"That depends..."

"On what?" she asked.

"On whether or not you'll marry me," he answered.

Dottie knew he was going to ask this. Still the shock of actually hearing the words surprised her. She dropped her salad fork. It ricocheted off her plate noisily. Now embarrassment added to her other feelings and she didn't know how to respond. So she burst out laughing.

"I'm not joking," Josh said. "I'm serious."

"Darling...I know you are. I'm sorry—it's just that you took me by surprise."

"Well—?" he asked once she had regained her composure.

"Josh," she said softly, "if you want an answer now—based on how I feel—I'd say *yes*, right now. But what happens to people who get married simply on feelings? There has to be more. There has to be something besides emotions to tell a person."

Dottie looked at him intently. "I mean," she continued, "I wish God could write a note, or something, and float it down to me for sure. Something this important has to be decided on the basis of whether it's God's will."

"I agree," Josh nodded. "Have you ever used the 'sound mind' principle to see if something is God's will?" he asked.

"How do you do that?"

"Well, you take a sheet of paper and divide it. On one side, you write down every reason why you *should* marry me. On the other side, you put down every reason why you *shouldn't*. Your answer will be very logical and clear."

That's just like a man, Dottie thought, *taking the romance out of a moment like this to make it "logical."*

CHAPTER
FIFTEEN

Nothing more was said about marriage. The couple finished dinner, continuing in conversation about other matters.

As Josh dropped her off at her apartment, she confessed, "I really can't tell you tonight. Let me pray about it some more...sleep on it."

Dottie woke up before dawn. She had a brief quiet time with the Lord, read from her Bible, then reached in her desk drawer for a sheet of paper. She made two columns: "Reasons to Marry Josh" and "Reasons Not to Marry Josh."

She reflected over the kind of person he was, listing on the favorable side his spiritual qualities and Christlikeness. She thought about the kind of husband he'd make—the kind of father he'd be.

As she thought about his ministry, which involved a great deal of travel, it was not as negative a consideration as it might have been for someone else. It was almost as if her father had prepared her for such a life with his own many moves while Dottie was growing up.

She thought, *How can I measure our attraction for one another?* Was it physical, spiritual, emotional? It occurred to her that it was all of these. Dottie recalled Josh's message on love, sex and marriage at Arrowhead Springs, after which she prayed for a man who had the same values as the speaker.

Was God giving her the speaker?

Dottie looked at her list. The column "for" was long with a number of reasons. The column "against" was limited to a few frivolous excuses.

Then she caught her breath. It was almost as if she heard God speak to her. *This is the paper you wanted to float down from heaven from Me with My answer. This is My will—not just your emotions.*

Josh came over later that morning for breakfast. Nothing significant was discussed. Soon it was getting close to lunch. Then he'd have to leave to catch a plane for his next assignment.

At 3:15 they were driving down Riverside Boulevard in Austin.

"Well..." Dottie began, "getting back to our

conversation of last night...do you know when your schedule for this year will be finalized?''

"That all depends," Josh said. "Will you marry me?''

"Yes," she replied simply.

Josh nearly swerved the car as he slammed on the brakes. He stopped the car in the middle of the boulevard, and while other autos passed on both sides, honking wildly, Josh kissed Dottie long and passionately.

"Let's go look for a ring," he exclaimed.

"Do we have time before your plane?''

"We'll take time.''

At the jewelry store they found one they really liked, but it was a couple sizes too large. Knowing it would probably take a week or two to have it sized properly, Dottie was disappointed. Now that her mind was made up, it was *really* made up.

The jeweler smiled at the couple. "Tell you what," he said, "if you want that ring, I'll size it for you. Come back in an hour and you can pick it up."

The happy pair walked excitedly along the river. They stopped to soberly reflect at what they were committing to, read from Josh's Bible, and prayed for God's blessing on their decision.

CHAPTER SIXTEEN

"WHY DID YOU WAIT SO LONG TO GET MARRIED?" A
FRIEND ASKED JOSH. "Did it take all that time to find the
right person?"

Josh noted the good-natured grin behind the
question, but did not treat it as lightly as it had been asked.
He replied thoughtfully, "I waited until I was 31 to get
married, not so much because I wanted to find the right
person...but rather, because it took *me* that long to become
the right person for a woman. I knew if I wanted to marry a
queen, I'd have to have the qualities of a king. I wasn't ready
for that kind of responsibility before now."

At Washington University a similar line of
questioning resulted from a discussion between Josh and a
university senior named Tom.

"I really appreciated what you had to say in your
lecture on sex, love and marriage," Tom said. "You'll be glad
to know that I have similar standards." Tom took out a
Seven Star diary he carried with him and read some 14
qualities he had listed for the woman he would marry.

"Tom," Josh asked him, "how do *you* measure up
to those 14 qualities? Are you loving, patient, self-controlled,
truthful. Do you spend enough time with the Lord?"

The student hesitated, then stammered,
"Ah...I...no, I...I guess not."

"Well, concentrate on developing those Christlike
qualities in your own life. Then trust God to give you a
woman who measures up to them as well."

Before their own wedding, Josh and Dottie went to
a Christian psychologist in Pennsylvania whose speciality was
marriage counseling. Each of them took tests to determine the

potential strengths and weaknesses of a marriage relationship.

The psychologist sat down with the couple and explained the results.

"These tests show some obvious differences in personality between the two of you," he said. "Dottie, your test results tell me that you'd like to have Josh to yourself...away from crowds. Alone. That's exactly opposite of your score, Josh. Your tests show a desire to be with people. You enjoy being part of the crowd. Now, each of you is going to have to give in, be flexible, to the other...or, you're going to have problems," he warned.

The tests brought out other facts and personality traits in each other that they hadn't yet discovered, and the knowledge helped them understand who they were marrying—and their marriage got off to a good start.

They were married in May and honeymooned in Mexico for three weeks. This was convenient for Josh's next assignment. Immediately following their honeymoon, Josh was to be dean of the "Institute for Biblical Studies" sponsored by Campus Crusade in Latin America.

Dottie went along on a tour of Mexico City with Josh and a busload of IBS students. Before the tour, Josh picked up a local guide book of some 150 pages. Dottie watched Josh speed-read the book just before the tour group departed. Although it looked to her as though he had simply browsed through the book in several minutes' time, he had apparently memorized its content!

As the bus toured the city, Josh narrated a running commentary, from memory, of the historic sites and background.

"Over there is the chapel of San Felipe, built in 1786 by Spanish missionaries," he explained. "The Chapel is the only building that remains of the original settlement. That winepress and mill that you see off to the left was part of the original Chapel. They are both in operation after nearly 200 years of use."

There's no way a person can do that, Dottie thought. *He must be making things up as he goes along.* She took out the guide book, thumbed through its pages to where they were, and discovered Josh was *not* bluffing. All the facts, dates and information were correct. Dottie was

CHAPTER
SIXTEEN

astounded at the mental capabilities of this man she had married.

Following the summer with Crusade's IBS program in Mexico, Josh and Dottie moved into a small apartment in Dallas. It was his first real "home" in over 10 years.

Josh's ministry began to grow and develop as he toured American campuses, speaking out for Christianity, debating Marxists and other radicals.

As he began to build a marriage and home, he found it necessary to also think about building an organization—a team to help him with the ever-growing demands of the ministry.

The first question he had to answer concerned the structure of his organization.

A number of people had encouraged him to resign from Crusade and establish his own ministry. Others had left the organization when they felt restricted by Crusade's policies and structure.

Or, perhaps they left because God had called them to a new ministry that seemed to be out of the strategy of Crusade's master plan for global evangelism. Dick Day was one of these. He loved working on campuses, and continually saw great evangelistic results from his Crusade ministry. But he saw God had given him the gifts of a pastor-teacher. So he left Crusade staff to concentrate on that aspect of his gifts. Dick was burdened at a secular world view which was having an increasing influence on Christians and the church leadership. From the searching of young people within cults, fads, experimentation with drugs and sex, Dick saw a widespread "falling away" among Christians—even in the lives of Christian leaders. He wanted to set up a center to deal with the problems of a Christian culture affected by worldly, secular views. He, Hal Lindsey, Bill Counts and Linus Morris, began a center for study, "The Light and Power House" in West Los Angeles.

Josh chose to stay with Campus Crusade, however.

"God called me to Crusade," he said simply, "and He hasn't called me to leave staff. There's no organization that can work as well as Crusade in follow-up of my campus ministry. The results would have far less impact if Crusade campus directors weren't able to say, 'He's one of us'. Crusade has given me my platform," he added, "and besides, I can't think of another Christian leader I'd rather work under than Bill Bright."

The question would be asked periodically again and again over the next few years, but once resolved, Josh refused to consider the other option of going out on his own.

Josh saw as the major consideration for building a team the simple fact of human limitations and restrictions of time and talent.

He recalled the difficult time he had in starting out as a speaker. He had vowed then that if he'd ever be in the position to help someone else get started, he'd do so.

The time had come to make good on his promise.

He reasoned that what had taken him nearly a decade to achieve might be duplicated by someone else in just three or four years, with his help to guide them past the pitfalls.

He had prayed early in his ministry, "Lord, I never want to do anything in my work which is not Your will. Sometimes I might be convinced that something is good and I ought to do it. But if it isn't Your will, the ministry will get bogged down and I might get tangled up in unwholesome motives, pride or something else. So, as a means of confirming Your will, whenever You give me the conviction to step out and do something, then I pray that You will give someone else—who has the ability to help me—the same conviction and bring us together. I want that to be a guiding principle in my ministry."

One of the first ones to respond to that guideline developed between Josh and the Lord was a hard-working, bright and energetic young man from California. Wes Ogg had worked under Dick Day on Crusade staff, directing the work at the Cal State-Long Beach campus. After two years, Wes was promoted to Area Administrator. It was in this assignment that Wes observed Josh and the growing pace of his ministry.

"He's going to 'burn out' before he's 40 if he doesn't get some help," Wes observed to Dick Day. "Josh does everything in his ministry. He makes the phone calls, handles the correspondence, packs the books, carries everything with him, sets up his own sound system and types his own correspondence. He should be doing things that are unique gifts God has given him. The routine things can be— and should be—done by others.''

Wes approached Josh offering his skills in administration. It was a specific answer to Josh's prayers for help. He had had a young man, Tom Stevens, who helped Josh with the ever-growing logistics of his schedule. But Tom had been accepted for seminary training and Josh needed someone who could do even more than replace Tom. He needed someone who could analyze his goals and strategies and help guide his dreams into tangible results.

Before Tom Stevens went off to seminary, Wes traveled extensively with him to learn every aspect of the organization and ministry. He assumed a new role of administrator for Josh so that Josh could concentrate on building the next level of his team concept. It was in this area, too, that Wes played a key function. Together, he and Josh laid the base for an important new media outreach. Josh saw films and TV programs as a means of expanding his outreach while at the same time freeing up some of his time.

Wes and Josh opened an office for Josh McDowell Ministries in Dallas.

In response to Josh's prayers to send someone if the idea was consistent with God's will, Carroll Nyquist of Johnson/Nyquist Films approached him with the concept of a film, ''What's Up, Josh?,'' which would be the first in a series of projects to be produced. Then Billy Zeoli, president of Gospel Films, offered to handle distribution of the films. In the process, Zeoli became a supportive friend of Josh and Dottie, often phoning with encouragement or other, more tangible, help.

As a result of the films and continuing exposure of his book, *Evidence That Demands a Verdict,* Josh was receiving many more invitations to speak than he could handle. They were mostly from campus leaders and churches who needed the kind of ministry Josh does well—classroom encounters, rallies, debates and lectures. A film or book, while helpful to some audiences, was not able to fit these

JOSH

needs. Though films and books could multiply Josh's effectiveness tremendously, he was still operating at the peak of his limitations—both as to time and health. It was obvious he needed to "reproduce" himself for the campus lecture ministry.

Ron Ralston, Crusade director on the Campus of Indiana University, approached Josh one day. "Josh," he said, "you're crazy to lead this kind of life. Why don't you train some other guys to help you?"

The next day, Josh went to Ron. "Dottie and I have been talking and praying about what you said yesterday. Ron, maybe God gave you that idea because *you're* the person to help me. Will you pray about it? I need someone to travel with me for a year and become that person you talked about."

Ron laughed. "No way, man! You couldn't get me to live the 'Samsonite' life. God is blessing my work here. Besides, I plan to go to graduate school and get a degree in public speaking and communications."

But Ron did agree to pray about it. And as he did so, God seemed to give him insight into areas he had not considered. Working with Josh would give him a more practical education in the field of speaking and communications. What better program could he find than on-the-job training in exactly his area of interest?

Ron later talked with Josh. "Is that option still available to travel with you?"

"I've been praying that you'd change your mind and come with me," Josh answered.

Josh also challenged another man to travel with him. Don Stewart was a student at Talbot Seminary and wanted a speaking ministry similar to Josh's.

Both Ron and Don became Josh's first interns, traveling with him cross-country and learning by doing.

Each took extensive notes. They listened to and watched their mentor in action.

Don observed as Josh kept the same pace as he had when first starting a ministry on U.S. university campuses. There would be breakfast meetings, classroom lectures, luncheon talks, radio or TV interviews, followed by the major lecture or rally at night. In the motel room, from eleven at

CHAPTER
SIXTEEN

night until two in the morning, Josh would conduct the business details, or work on his book manuscript, while waiting to "wind down" from the energized schedule. Then, at seven a.m., it began all over again.

At the airport, between flights, Josh would get as many as 20 quick phone calls in while the interns checked in their baggage and took care of seat assignments. On the planes, Josh penned short notes to his financial supporters and autographed books for prayer partners.

The interns helped with the sound equipment, book tables and other details. As they traveled with Josh, in addition to picking up skills of speaking and how to handle an audience, he taught them some of the "nuts and bolts" principles of communications—things not usually found in the textbooks.

Ron and Don also picked up on other skills and attitudes which were not so much taught as caught. These were Josh's spiritual attitudes and qualities.

On one occasion, a sponsoring organization had problems because they had not done their homework. The proper preparation had not been done, and things had not gone well as a result. The director, in turn, took things out on Josh—blaming him for mistakes that he himself had made.

Ron Ralston was angry as he heard the man berating Josh. "You were insensitive to our staff people," the director complained. "You should have spent more time with the staff, telling them what was expected."

Ron knew all of that was thoroughly covered in the correspondence and a manual that was sent months earlier. Because there would be no time for such briefings once Josh got to the campus, they knew such things had to be covered in advance. Ron waited for Josh to say, "You just didn't do your homework, you lunkhead."

Instead he heard, "I'm sorry. You're right. It's my fault and I apologize," Josh told the campus leader.

Seldom did they see Josh react in an unwholesome way to a situation. His attitudes were always proper, although sometimes misunderstood. He often asked for something to be done over if it was wrong or done sloppily. He had no tolerance for poor quality work. If he seemed insensitive to others' feelings on this matter, it was not meant as a personal rebuke as much as a challenge to perfection.

The discipline of serving as interns was not easy. The two men toured for a year with Josh almost as his servants, to be trained to do what he was doing so well. It was a difficult standard to attain.

After a year of traveling with him, Josh asked Ron, "What are your plans for the coming year?"

"Oh, man," Ron exclaimed, "I've learned so much this year—but probably the greatest thing I learned is how much I *don't* know. I really feel inadequate. I've been thinking of traveling with you another year."

"No," Josh shook his head. "I think you should go out on your own to speak. Travel on university campuses yourself."

Ron laughed. It was a *most* premature idea.

But Josh was serious.

"I can't do it yet," Ron protested. "I've only talked *once* all year."

"That doesn't matter. You have what it takes. I'm counting on you to help relieve my load next year."

"I'll pray about it," Ron said.

Josh sent Ron to two university campuses that fall. At these, Ron learned he could speak. God blessed his efforts, as Ron told Josh, "not because I was so good—but because I was obedient."

"Agreed," said Josh. "And you'll see Him bless even more as you trust Him for the results. You stay faithful."

Both Ron and Don Stewart began to travel on their own and speak. They learned firsthand the emotional as well as physical demands of the rigorous assignment. As each of them encountered a difficult or uncomfortable situation, they tried to think how their teacher would have reacted and tried to respond accordingly.

For two years, while a student at Sacramento State College, young Pat Hurley had a dream. He got his chance to express it in person when Josh visited his campus. Shyly he confessed, "Mr. McDowell, I want to do what you're doing. I have a dream of doing it, but in high schools across the

CHAPTER
SIXTEEN

country.''

Pat had asked for the chance to drive Josh to the airport after his engagement at his university. That way he could get some advice from the one person who could help him most.

"I'm working in a local church as a youth pastor. But I want to be a high school speaker," Pat said.

"And you'd like my advice?" Josh asked.

"Yeah!" Pat exclaimed. "How can I have a ministry like yours?"

"Be filled with the Holy Spirit," Josh replied. Then, as if to read Pat's thoughts, he said, "You were expecting some formula...a secret plan. But what God wants are guys he can trust and eventually use."

Pat later reflected over Josh's challenge. *I know God's called me to speak to high school kids in the same way He's called Josh to speak on university campuses. But I'll never accomplish anything unless I get my life together the way Josh has...unless I work as hard as he does.*

In a phone call to Josh, Pat asked if these thoughts were correct.

"That's true," Josh told him. "You can't make it on the basis of talent alone. The Holy Spirit makes it happen. You see, Pat, I don't think God ordains personalities—He uses people with character."

After an intensive one-week session with Josh in Portland and later regular phone calls for advice and counsel, Pat stepped out on faith with a high school ministry similar to Josh's even using much of Josh's apologetic research and notes.

"Man, I'm excited for you!" Josh told Pat. "Think about it, Pat...we can *change the world* with Jesus Christ. Isn't that an exciting thought. Go out there and *do* it!''

Through the years, Dick Purnell—Josh's Wheaton College roommate—had stayed in touch with his friend. Initially, they were surprised to see that God had independently called each to Campus Crusade for Christ. After several years of Crusade ministry, Dick went back to school to study for the ministry. He was both surprised and impressed to see his old friend, Josh, at his graduation from Trinity Seminary in Deerfield, Illinois. Dick took a church assignment in Bloomington, Indiana, where he became pastor to 350 college students who came to hear him on Sunday morning.

For several years he ministered at the church, watching it grow. Meanwhile Josh periodically reappeared to tell his old friend of a higher potential. "Each week you preach to several hundred people," Josh told Dick. "But you ought to have a national platform. More people need to hear what you're saying." Finally, Dick himself saw the truth in Josh's words. He resigned from his church to work full time with Josh, going out first under the auspices of Josh's non-profit organization, then rejoining the Crusade staff as a national speaker.

Two brothers from Ohio, David and Dale Bellis, approached Josh with a dream of theirs. "There's a dramatic need in churches for your material," Dave Bellis told Josh and Wes Ogg in their first meeting together. "The films are helpful...and so are your books," Dave explained, "but what the churches need is a concentrated seminar that could give many hours of material to Christians—similar to what you do on university campuses, but aimed at Christians primarily, and presented live."

"How do you see this working?" Wes asked.

Before Dave could answer, Josh chimed in, "Right now I'm so busy on campuses, how could I speak to the number of churches you're talking about?"

Dale Bellis spoke up. "Instead of having you go into one church and speak to several hundred people, we'll rent larger facilities—civic auditoriums or convention centers—so we can attract audiences of 5,000."

"It would be promoted and advertised as a city-wide cooperative event," Dave added. "It would have multi-media graphics, manuals, proper teaching techniques and support materials."

The Bellis' contracted with Quadrus Communications in Rockford, Illinois, to produce television

CHAPTER
SIXTEEN

"clips"—animation, dramatic vignettes, graphics and other illustrations—which were put on a videotape and projected on large screens to augment Josh's six hours of lecture materials.

The concept took nearly a year to launch, but it became an immediate success in the test cities where it was tried.

As Wes Ogg became more involved with the long-range planning and development of the Josh McDowell Ministry, it became apparent that the organization needed a person with administrative skills to come to Dallas and manage the growing staff and office operations.

Loren Lillestrand, a Crusade national team member at Arrowhead Springs, heard that one of his top area administrators was growing restless and needed a new challenge. Bob Tiede had become a Christian through Crusade, and had gone on staff three years later. He and his wife, Sherry, had been Crusade directors at two universities out west. Loren had Bob fly to Dallas and look at Josh's work. Neither Wes nor Josh knew Bob, but invited him to their office and operations.

"It's incredible all that they're doing there," Bob Tiede reported back to Loren. "Wes and Josh are really sharp."

"But did you see how you'd fit in?" Loren asked.

"Me? Well, sure. They could use my help, but—"

"Will you pray about joining them?"

"No...I won't even pray about it," Bob replied. "You see, I think anyone who goes into that work should do so because *Josh wants them to*—not because they're assigned. You could assign me to go, but if it wasn't a situation where Josh saw the need and asked for help, it wouldn't work."

"That's true of most personnel situations," Loren admitted, "but you don't know Josh."

"Sorry," Bob interrupted. "Josh has to see the need and ask for help—*then* I'll pray about it."

A month later, Josh did call. "I want to fly you and Sherry to Dallas...I want you to think seriously about joining us."

The welcome was warm and genuine. Dottie and

Sherry felt as if they were lifelong friends after just 20 minutes of chatting.

On the plane back after their visit to Dallas, Bob was thinking out loud. "I was reading in the book of Acts how the apostles were neglecting their ministry because of the details of administration and prayed for godly men to come and help them. Do you think I could be useful to Josh in this way?"

Sherry nodded. "I think we ought to go," she said simply.

Bob called Josh to accept his offer, rented a Ryder truck and set out with their three small children for the 2,000-mile trip to Texas. Josh and Dottie met Bob and Sherry when the truck pulled up to their new house. The McDowells had brought a bucket of fried chicken and pitched in to help them unload the truck and unpack.

Once settled, Bob eagerly dug into his new responsibilities. He had directed the "I Found It" campaign in Yakima, Washington, and supervised the 900 volunteer workers. He enjoyed making order out of chaos, and began setting up the systems and organization of the administration for Josh's offices.

Ethan Pope came to Christ through Crusade ministry at the University of Mississippi. Torn between a business career and Christian work, he decided to work with Campus Crusade.

Assigned to Auburn University, Ethan's work was noticed by his regional director. Dan Hayes asked Ethan, "Josh McDowell desperately needs an advance man to precede him on campuses around the country and help set up the arrangements for his coming to speak. Will you pray about taking this on?"

Ethan went to Dallas and worked for about eight months on the advance work. But more and more he saw a greater need, and approached Josh one day to tell him about it.

"At this time I feel God is calling me full time into the area of fund raising and development. The greatest opportunities for ministry, for me, are in the area of finances. It

CHAPTER
SIXTEEN

takes money for a ministry to succeed, and I think God has someone else in mind for advance work," he told Josh.

Josh looked disappointed. He was thinking, *I'm really sorry to be losing you, Ethan. I've really admired the work you've done for me.*

"But," Ethan added, "I'm not *leaving*. I'm asking for a transfer. I feel God is calling me to work for *you* in the area of public relations, fund raising and development. I've watched you. I believe you spend a third of your time trying to raise money for the ministry...and PR duties. Trying to find and cultivate donors takes you away from your primary gift of speaking. I want to help."

"I see that as an answer to prayer," Wes Ogg concurred. "I think we should sit down and come up with a public relations and fund raising strategy and put Ethan in charge."

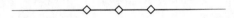

Josh's team was augmented by a number of others over the past ten years.

Warren Culwell, a graduate of the University of Texas, took a year before entering seminary to be a personal assistant to Josh. That year stretched to two as Josh came to rely on Warren more and more. Acting as personal assistant Warren returns phone calls and handles as much business as he can to free up precious moments for Josh.

On the road, Warren and Josh get adjoining motel rooms. While Josh is talking long distance on the telephone in one room, Warren is on the phone in the other room placing another call. The two of them go back and forth that way until well after midnight if they're on the East Coast, since it is still only nine o'clock in California.

Like others who traveled with Josh, Warren resented what he felt were unjustified criticisms of Josh. Some sponsors accused Josh of being a prima donna because he didn't devote all his time to them. "If they only knew the truth of Josh's heart, as I do," Warren observed, "they wouldn't be critical."

Lois Wesolek became an unofficial member of Josh's team early in his ministry. She became his "adopted" mother. She worried about his health and sent vitamins to him on the road, knowing that he probably wasn't eating properly and getting the right amount of rest.

Before he was married, Josh often stayed in their home when based in California. Following his marriage, when he traveled through California, their home became his "base."

It was Lois who helped with his early mailings and prayer letters. She was also the one who proposed receptions as fund-raisers for Josh's TV specials. Lois hosted one in her home for Los Angeles and it became the prototype for an approach for other cities.

When her husband was dying of cancer, Josh was to give his testimony at a Billy Graham Crusade in San Diego. When he heard the news, he canceled his appearance and rushed back to comfort Lois.

At Campus Crusade, in addition to Bill Bright, there were other key leaders who helped Josh develop or maintain an ongoing ministry: Loren Lillestrand, Roger Randall, Rodney "Swede" Anderson, and Robbie Gowdey were among those who contributed.

Looking back, whether for advertising, publicity, fund raising, administration, advance work, films, television, seminars, cassette tapes, books or other aspects of the ministry, Josh recalls having the conviction for many of these and praying for God to lead to their fulfillment. In each instance, God directed a person to come forward, at His time, with an offer of help.

IN SPITE OF THE FACT THAT JOSH WAS DEVELOPING A TEAM TO ASSIST HIM, to give him an opportunity to reach more people, his workload did not decrease.

Especially on the road, even with interns to run interference for him, pulling him out of meetings that tended to run too long, Josh was running ragged.

"I only need five minutes," someone would say. Usually that meant a half hour. And that "someone" would be followed by another someone, and another until Josh was talking with people until the middle of the night.

Josh took the problem to Dick Day, who was becoming his "Barnabas"—one who could always be counted on to look after Josh's best interests.

"Why do you feel so responsible?" he asked Josh. "Besides, you might be robbing someone else of the joy of counseling someone in spiritual need. You don't have to talk to every person who has a spiritual need, you know. You've got to learn how to say 'no'—for your own good, and for the sake of your family."

Josh made it one of his goals to work on that area of his life. Goals were an important part of his ministry. He had seen so many others with a creative vision or idea fizzle or fall apart because they had no strategy for implementing their idea.

That is why he appreciated Campus Crusade, with Bill Bright's emphasis on planning. By setting objectives, he discovered, a person accomplishes as much as possible. "Faith is trusting God to make the most of what *you do,*" he told his interns.

JOSH

"My overall goal is to go to heaven and take as many people with me as I can," he often said.

To give purpose to his plans, Josh often works with a large map of the world before him. "What I'm doing can change my world," he reminds himself. The significance of that is borne out in the lives of those he reaches on university campuses—engineers, technicians, surgeons, ministers. They are the people of influence in the next generation. They will be going to all corners of the earth—China, Africa, Russia, South America, Europe. Josh's prayer is that he can influence them to come to Christ, then motivate them to take the gospel with them wherever they go.

With that premise as his guiding purpose, Josh recalls one of his earliest principles: "I'm going to talk to people about Christ unless the Holy Spirit tells me not to."

Josh more or less expected other people to have the same spirit of boldness. He and Dottie were having dinner at a Japanese steak house in Houston. Their dinner companions included a woman Crusade staff member, and her date, John Blevin, a graduate student.

"What are you studying, John?" Josh asked him.

"Medicine," was the reply.

"Oh," Josh said, "missionary medicine, right?"

"Uh...no...." John said.

"But you're a Christian—you're not enrolled in the study of missionary medicine?"

"No," John answered, "but I've told God that if He opened the door, I'd go."

"What are you saying?" Josh asked in mock disbelief. "There are thousands of doors open! They're open *wide,* John. Everywhere I go I run into missionaries who tell me about clinics they run. They've been praying for *years* for God to send them a Christian doctor."

Then Josh introduced him to his philosophy. "John, why don't you tell God, 'Lord, I'm going to serve You as a full-time medical missionary unless You close the door. If You *don't* want me to go, then *You* close the door.' "

"That sounds interesting. I've never heard that before."

"Neither did I until I read the Bible. Look at the Apostle Paul. He didn't say to the Romans, 'Maybe, if the

CHAPTER
SEVENTEEN

doors open, I'll stop by there some day.' No...he said, 'I keep trying to come, but God keeps closing the door.' And what was the last thing our Lord said before ascending into heaven?''

"All right—I get the picture."

" 'Go ye into all the world'—not, 'Just take it easy until I open the door for you.' "

"Okay, okay," John laughed. "I give up. You've made your point."

"Good," Josh grinned.

"But you ought to be careful coming on so strong. Somebody might punch you out for being so bold!''

Josh's approach to his work has the same degree of audacious commitment—he works hard and assumes everyone else has both the motivation and energy level. When people come up to him after meetings and say, "I wish I had the time to write books and do all the things you do," he has a simple answer.

"You do have the time," he says. "It's a matter of priorities. I work hard, but I don't have any more time than you do. We each have 24 hours in a day. It's how I use my time that counts." The words seem harsh, but they are said in a matter-of-fact tone without the sound of judging. To Josh, it's simply a matter of stating a fact.

Because Josh is always working, he isn't always sensitive that not everyone has his capacity or energy. He sometimes calls people at very late hours or extra early hours without apology. There are some who resent such "intrusions," others are hurt when he asks for help on a day off, holiday or other free time. When he is working, he assumes that everyone else is, too. Instead they feel he is using them as he sometimes feels used when his speaking schedule is abused.

However, Dottie is a source of balance and reminds him from time to time to separate the work and social or free times of others.

Further, he makes a point of telling all new personnel, "Look, I have a problem in not being sensitive to people's needs sometimes. When I make demands of you...cut you off...or am unreasonable to you, you have a responsibility to tell me. And I'll back off and apologize. Fair enough?''

JOSH

To be able to speak on campuses and hold a crowd, his talks have to have substance. To prepare, Josh reads some 300 books a year. In addition to this load, his research assistant, Mark Lundeen, goes through scores of periodicals each month and provides Josh with a digest of material.

The nearest thing to relaxation and a hobby for Josh is working in the yard or stripping the finish off antique furniture. Likewise, he never takes a vacation just for the sake of rest. He always ties it in with speaking engagements.

He is intense and spends approximately 1½ to 2 hours in preparation for each minute of every new talk he gives. Using his basic material as an outline, Josh looks for ways to make his presentation current and vital by giving fresh or unique applications of the content to the audience to whom it is addressed.

There is always the temptation to tamper with the message—to make it more profound, more theological. Dr. Bright warned Josh, "You're going to be pressured by ministers or professors and others to give 'more depth' to your talks on the resurrection and other topics. But stick to the basics. People will be more responsive. If you get more complicated trying to sound more profound, you'll only be reaching a few of your peers and feeding your ego. By sticking to the basics, though, you'll be reaching thousands, maybe millions. Stick to the basics."

With so many hours of preparation, prayer and thought going into the one-hour talk, Josh finds it difficult to "wind down" afterwards, so usually writes, reads or works on other business until about two in the morning.

He knows when he speaks that he is prepared. That is why, usually 40 minutes before the talk, he likes to mingle with people in the audience. On campuses, he learns who potential radicals or trouble makers are. Or, in other instances, he gets a personal sense of the audience need by talking to 20 or 30 people and learning their names and concerns.

In churches, Josh sometimes appears to be disconcerting to pastors who want him to join them in the perfunctory "prayer meeting with the deacons."

"I'm 'all prayed up,'" Josh tells them. "I've been praying for this meeting for a long time. Besides, it's too late

CHAPTER
SEVENTEEN

to start now. I'd like to go out and meet people and get a sense of their needs. Go ahead and pray for the meeting without me.''

Some groups inadvertently take advantage of Josh's energy and desire to see spiritual results.

In Springfield, Massachusetts, he spoke for 13 straight hours. At Buffalo University, he gave 14 speeches in one day, beginning at 6:00 a.m. and concluding near midnight.

Josh blames himself for the fact that such things happen, since he still has difficulty in saying "no."

Warren Culwell observes, "Josh would not be where he is today if it were not for the lessons learned early in his ministry—the lesson of being a servant."

People who schedule Josh aren't always aware that he comes to them having just completed a rigorous speaking schedule. They assume he's rested, fresh and ready to be used. Like any good businessman, they want to amortize their expenses wisely.

The grind of being on the road has its dehumanizing aspect, too. Sleeping in different motels every week, traveling from one campus to the next, Josh is often thought of as simply providing a service for which he is paid.

"I simply can't speak one more time," Josh might complain. "I'm spent—exhausted."

"But," the sponsor protests, "we're *paying* over $1,000 for you to be here this week. That's $200 a day! And you can't speak for just one more hour?"

Such a rationale makes Josh feel cheap, as if he is prostituting himself and his message because a price tag is put on his services.

Dick Day, ever the encourager, reminds Josh, "It goes back to your motivations. Are you doing this to be accepted—to be concerned about what people say about you? Or are you doing it to win people to Jesus Christ? You can say 'no' to people if your motive is to serve Christ. Don't worry about what they think. Let the Lord handle that for you."

Unfortunately, Josh puts undue pressure on himself. Perhaps it comes from his allegiance to Crusade, churches and other Christian organizations, where the emphasis is often put unwittingly on performance. Reports wanting to know how many he spoke to, how often, and what happened, upset the proper balance. "In order to prove myself worthy to others, I thought I had to out-perform everyone else," he confesses.

There are times, too, when he sees his office staff and equipment—the cost of overhead—and worries, "What if I get sick?" At other times the pressure is so intense he'd like to get away from it all for awhile.

On the road for so many years without his own apartment meant he had no personal retreat for needed rest. Even when he traveled, he had no privacy in those early days. To save a $15 a night motel bill, Josh would stay in houses. Usually, it was with the campus director and his wife. They were always willing to talk—to share spiritual truths—until early in the morning. And, in the morning, Josh—who slept on the sofa—had to be up earliest, so they wouldn't catch him in his BVD's. Nor could he sleep in. He always left in the morning with the director. He didn't want to convey any wrong impressions by staying alone in a house with a woman.

In the early days, he couldn't afford Holiday Inns, so if there wasn't a home to stay in, he'd sleep at a skid row flophouse for two dollars a night.

Because of his travels to South America and across the United States, Josh had little time to develop friendships. He had only a handful of real friends, although he had thousands of acquaintances.

The friends he does have—like Paul Lewis, Dick Purnell, Dick Day and a few others—are treasured.

When someone accused Josh of being proud and arrogant, he confided in Dick Purnell. "Is it true? Am I that way?"

"No," Dick smiled. "It might come off that way to someone who doesn't know you. But it's not arrogance. It's self-confidence. I don't know anyone more self-confident than you. It's because you've worked hard—you've struggled through the problems looking for strategies, and found them. You know what works and what doesn't. When you try to show this to other people, they think you're being rigid, bullheaded. Arrogant."

Paul Lewis explained another misunderstanding.

CHAPTER
SEVENTEEN

"People think your convictions are unusual—that you're special. That's probably because most people don't have any convictions of their own. They're bothered that you seem so sure of yourself—they mistake your confidence as ego and pride."

Curiously, Josh has more of a problem with people who praise him than criticize him. "People give me credit for things I don't do. It rightfully belongs to the Lord—and, humanly speaking—to a lot of hard-working staff people. Dave and Dale Bellis do all the work for the 'Six Hours With Josh McDowell' seminars, but I come in and everyone credits *me* with it." He would prefer that the glory go rightfully to God.

Josh weighs criticism carefully. He asks, "Does the person criticizing demonstrate in his life the spiritual qualities that give him the right to criticize?"

Most criticism, Josh discovered, comes from Christians, not unbelievers. Usually it comes from not knowing the facts and jumping to erroneous conclusions. Other times, criticism is based on false rumors.

"Josh is only interested in money," one Christian leader said. Actually, the opposite is true. If a group isn't able to make their budget, as often as not he will make up the difference somehow. Also, some think if Josh charges $500 for a day, that he, personally, is getting the money. The fact is, he must pay his own expenses, as well as the one or two assistants who travel with him. Often, he loses money on an assignment.

Another criticism says, "Josh is making a fortune on cassette tapes and book royalties." The truth is, he sells the tapes for twenty cents over his cost and often gives them to students who can't afford to pay. Again, it is often a losing financial project. The royalties from his books go to Campus Crusade for Christ.

His only paid income is the modest support he draws as a Crusade staff member. Even then he raises it himself.

There are times when financial matters do become a problem with Josh. His humanity shows at such times and he usually has to grit his teeth. These are the times when a secular university's student union or administration will bring

JOSH

a well-known lecturer on campus for a one-night talk. Some of them, during the seventies, included convicted felons, drug advocates, witches and warlocks, terrorists and others whose stated purpose was to destroy the moral integrity and fabric of the country and its institutions. For this, they were paid fees ranging from $400 to $15,000 of taxpayers' money.

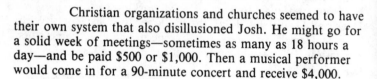

Christian organizations and churches seemed to have their own system that also disillusioned Josh. He might go for a solid week of meetings—sometimes as many as 18 hours a day—and be paid $500 or $1,000. Then a musical performer would come in for a 90-minute concert and receive $4,000.

It never seemed quite fair or a correct sense of stewardship to Josh.

Health is a problem for someone who is constantly on the road, not getting enough sleep, not always eating the right food.

Having had serious bouts with sickness in South America, Josh's body was more susceptible to sickness than it should have been.

Some matters he could deal with himself.

When he started out as a public speaker, if he spoke for an hour, he'd get hoarse. Since he spoke constantly, his voice was always on the threshold of hoarseness. Josh tried the typical home remedies—sucking lemons, cough drops, hot water and honey—and nothing seemed to work.

At the University of Texas, a young woman came up to him and said shyly, "Forgive me for telling you this—but you're breathing all wrong. Totally wrong."

"What do you mean?" he kidded. "I was born breathing this way."

"Yes, and you're going to destroy your voice," she warned.

"You're serious, aren't you?"

"I am...and I think I can help you."

"Tell me," he urged.

She told him he was breathing from his upper torso and not his diaphragm. "Try breathing this way," she said, demonstrating.

CHAPTER SEVENTEEN

"I thought that kind of breathing was only for singers," Josh remarked.

"Your lungs are for air to pass *through,* not *from.* When you breathe your way, you get only a little air in your chest. You take shallow, quick breaths. And as the air rushes back and forth across the vocal chords, it vibrates them and wears them down. It makes them raw. When you breathe from your diaphragm, letting the air pass *through* your lungs, you can speak with less effort and fatigue to your vocal chords."

It was true. After two years of practice, he mastered the breathing to the point where he can now talk for hours without strain to his voice.

Knowing his limits is Josh's key to effectiveness. He learned several years ago that he has a physical problem that affects his well-being. Josh noticed that at certain times, he would cave in from pressure—he would become irritable or curt with people. He attributed it to a lack of spirituality. So he began to pray more and spent more time in the Scriptures. It didn't help.

Then Dr. William Halcomb noticed what appeared to him to be symptoms of a physical cause. "Josh, come up and see me. I want to give you a glucose tolerance test."

In the doctor's office, Josh fell apart during the test.

"You have acute hypoglycemia," the doctor told him. "You need to get eight hours of sleep at night and eat something every two hours and keep up with your racquet ball—the exercise is good for you. If you don't follow this plan, you'll be irritable and jumpy—you'll lash out at people. Your entire personality will change. Remember, if you lose your temper, it probably isn't a spiritual problem. You just forgot to eat!"

With a proper diet and an adjustment to his sleeping and eating habits, Josh is able to control his hypoglycemia.

"For years I was intimidated by Bill Bright and Dr. Bright never knew it," Josh says. "Dr. Bright is able to function well on just a little sleep. So I thought I could live on four hours of sleep. But my metabolism needs more than that. For years I punished my body thinking everyone had that capacity."

JOSH

Other times, Josh allowed others, unknowingly, to punish his body. Some campus directors seemed insensitive to illness.

Once Josh was at a university speaking and got sick. He began to cough up blood. He immediately went to a doctor who diagnosed his problem as a serious sinus infection.

"I recommend you get on the next plane home and check into your own hospital, with your own doctor," he advised.

The director would not hear of it. "But you can't leave. What about all the money we've spent? Can't you leave in the morning? It isn't fair to all those people who are expecting you."

"But, I'm really sick," Josh complained. "I think we should cancel."

"One more talk won't hurt. We'll keep it short and you can go back to the hotel as soon as it's over."

Against his better judgment Josh gave in to the pressure.

Back at the hotel later, Josh was ready to go to the auditorium to speak, but no one came to pick him up. Josh had to take a taxi to get there on time. When he got there, a large crowd of 4,500 people were already waiting. But when he went inside, Josh learned the auditorium was actually an ice arena. The speaker's platform was a small riser on the center of the ice rink. The warm air in the stands acted like a blower and blew across the ice from all directions at Josh. By the time it reached him, it was thoroughly chilled. It was almost as if a giant fan was blowing cold air directly at him.

Josh spoke with difficulty, coughing up much blood and mucous. When he finished speaking, he nearly collapsed. Dizzy and weak, he went back to the hotel.

After a few hours of fitful sleep, Josh awoke to leave for a flight home to the hospital. Again, no one was there to pick him up and take him to the airport.

It took nearly six months for him to fully recover.

Not all sponsors are so insensitive, however.

Josh got sick while en route to a series of meetings at Bethany Church of the Nazarene in Bethany, Oklahoma. Dottie was with him in Washington, D.C., when Josh got quite ill.

CHAPTER
SEVENTEEN

"Honey, cancel the meetings," she begged. "You can't go, as sick as you are."

"Darling," he told her, "you don't understand the pressure they put on you. They've promoted this—spent a lot of money. They're counting on us. Besides, Pastor Gilliland has always been good to us."

Dottie did not give up. "Please...for my sake. Call him and see."

"All right." Josh walked to a nearby pay phone and called.

"Pastor Gilliland, I'm in Washington, D.C. and I'm sick with the flu...."

Without missing a beat, the minister said, "Josh, where are you now?"

"I'm with Dottie at National Airport."

"Well, you take Dottie and go straight home. We'll make it through all right. God must have something else in store for us."

Josh hung up the phone, wondering if he heard correctly.

"He said, 'okay—to go straight home and get well.'" Josh was impressed with the expression of Christian compassion and the minister's acceptance of the change as God's plan for them.

CHAPTER EIGHTEEN

DOTTIE TRAVELED WITH JOSH much of the time when they were first married. The first year they lived in a small apartment in Dallas.

Then, to be closer to Crusade headquarters, they moved to San Bernardino. They rented an apartment for the first year, since they were on the road for at least three weeks of the month. Then they bought a small Spanish style bungalow.

It was here that their first child, a daughter, was born. Kelly, as she was named, took to the road like a seasoned traveler.

Dottie had prayed for Kelly, even before she was conceived. "Lord," she said to God often, "we pray You will only give us children if they will come to You—receive Your Son as Savior—live for You in later life and be servants of Christ."

Josh had taken Dottie with him to the University of Minnesota when his life had been threatened. It was her first real confrontation with that fear. She was angry as well as frightened. She could not imagine why anyone would want to do him violence.

Josh does not frighten. He told her, "Honey, there's nothing to be afraid of. My life is in God's hand. I trust Him to protect me."

"But you have a way of meeting criticism head on," she said. "That's what frightens me."

By the mid-seventies, the threats had subsided some. Most of the radical student groups on campus were defunct. Josh no longer spoke out much on the errors of revolutionists.

JOSH

Now people reacted against Josh's strong morality stance. Threats on his life still persisted, but more often than not they came from angry guys whose girl friends stopped sleeping with them after hearing Josh speak out against sexual immorality.

A phone call came: "You wrecked my relationship—now I'm gonna destroy *your* home. Your family is as good as dead!"

The authorities were quickly called and the man picked up some two blocks from the McDowell house.

Threats of violence were also being replaced with attempts to compromise Josh. On three separate occasions students hired women to be nude and in his motel room following a speaking engagement. It was usually easy to gain access to his room—either by bribing a desk clerk or picking the lock. Somehow, they got in. The woman disrobed, while a photographer hid in the closet or bathroom, ready to "document" the event.

"If it ever happened to me even once," Josh said, "—my picture with a nude woman, I'd be finished. No one would ever believe me."

To insure that it never happened, Josh began taking interns and assistants with him. They always check out a room ahead of Josh for security.

Other attempts to compromise him have been tried, including times when someone would steal his attache or luggage, pick the lock, then put pornographic materials or drug paraphernalia inside, to embarrass him later.

Dottie tried to maintain Josh's attitude. It was true. They were in God's hand and their lives controlled by His sovereignty. She would "trust, and not be afraid."

In 1976, Josh and Dottie, along with two-year-old Kelly, moved back to Dallas. Texas was more central for a nationwide traveling ministry.

Josh was beginning also to build a team of associates to work with him. Wes Ogg helped Josh open an office in Richardson, a northern suburb of Dallas.

As the ministry began to grow, larger and larger crowds came out to hear Josh on campuses.

CHAPTER
EIGHTEEN

As their work grew, so did their unconscious attitudes toward the ministry. Bigger was better; more was best. It took a big letdown for God to teach Josh that His ways were different from ours.

Josh flew to Michigan to address a Crusade leadership training group, expecting to speak to several hundred people. Seven persons showed up. Josh was upset, "Look at that turnout. It's awful! My airfare and expenses are $350...$350 to teach seven people. What a waste of time."

The Spirit of God convicted Josh that these seven were as worthy of his best efforts as 700. Thus motivated, Josh spoke and God blessed his efforts. Today, three of the seven are full-time pastors, and more than 3,000 people have been won to Christ as a result of the witness of these seven.

One Christian worked at the Kellogg plant near Josh's hometown, in Battle Creek. This young believer noted there were over 360 people in his division. He said, "Josh, thanks for the principles you gave us in leadership training. I'm going back to work to reach my division for Christ. I sat down and figured if I spoke to a different person at each coffee break and lunch period, I'd be able to share Christ with everyone inside of a year."

After a year, the young man reached his goal. He had talked to every person in his division about Christ—and 83 of them prayed to receive Him as Saviour.

No longer did Josh expect God to work only in the major events. He was constantly being surprised and excited at the unexpected—the seemingly small.

Paul Lewis had taught a Crusade IBS course in Mexico on "The Christian Marriage and Family." He was convinced of the need for a book on dating and sex, especially for Christian single men.

Josh had been praying for God to send him someone who would work together with him on just such a book.

Armed with his own notes, plus transcripts of all Josh's messages on the subject, Paul put together the manuscript for a book.

JOSH

Each man drew from his own healthy marriage relationship.

Josh recalled when he and Dottie, as an engaged Christian couple, visited the marriage counselor for advice for their planned marriage. They each practiced the principles of bending to the other's needs.

But one area Josh worked on harder than others was communication. When he'd return from a trip, he'd be exhausted, and it was easy to "clam up." Never really adept at relating details, his conversations seemed as tedious as tooth extractions to Dottie.

"Did you see the Fullers on your trip?" she'd ask, trying to prime the pump of conversation.

"Uh-huh."

"Did you talk to them?"

"I talked to Ed. Sheila was in the hospital."

"The hospital? What's wrong?" Dottie asked.

"Nothing—she had a baby," Josh answered.

"A baby. How nice. Was it a boy or girl?"

"I didn't think to ask. I just congratulated Ed."

"Well, how much did it weigh—when was it born—what did they name it?" Dottie wanted to know.

"Honey, I don't know," Josh answered lamely.

Because Dottie is interested in such details, Josh now goes out of his way to learn them.

There is also another area to work on.

"Sweetheart," she told Josh, "you know...there's something you do that really bothers me."

"What do you mean, honey?" he asked.

"Sometimes you don't seem interested in the little things in my life. You're out on the road...out in the world...in all kinds of exciting things. You don't seem interested in my world back here at home and it hurts."

"I don't?" Josh said, putting down the paper.

"Like right now. At the table when you read the paper or a book. When I talk to you, your mind is somewhere else—probably on a free speech platform in Bolivia."

"Honey, you're the most important thing, after the Lord, in my life," he told her.

"But that isn't the message I'm getting. You communicate to me that I'm not so important as the

CHAPTER
EIGHTEEN

newspaper or magazine.''

He sat for a moment and thought about it. Then he put aside his paper. "Honey...I'm sorry. I'll try to work on it.''

Later, it was obvious to her that Josh was working at it. She threw her arms around him and kissed him. "Thank you for trying to communicate and be sensitive to my needs,'' she said.

As they worked out smoothness in their marriage, they learned to follow the ageless wisdom of not allowing the sun to go down on their wrath.

One time Josh was angry about something and went out to the car to leave for the airport. He came back in quickly, however, to make things right with Dottie before he left.

It happened again. This time he was a block away and drove back to correct the problem.

He got short with her on the phone one time and had to call back right away to apologize.

Phone calls are their means of staying in touch when Josh travels. It costs them a great deal for Josh to call her every night, but it is an investment well worth it.

When he thinks about his own marriage and how God prepared each of them for it, Josh is understandably concerned that others have the same thing.

When Pat Hurley, the Crusade speaker he encouraged to speak on high school campuses, was getting married, Josh phoned him.

"Do you remember our talk on the way to the airport?'' he asked Pat.

"Yeah, I do,'' he said. "I remember you explained how you had to break up with a girl in order to be in God's will.''

"Well, Pat, I just called to tell you to make sure...please make sure.'' Josh's voice was strained, tight. As Pat listened he could tell Josh had wrestled with whether he should call or not. He risked his friendship with Pat if he offended him, and he hated doing it, but felt compelled to do so.

"God's going to use you, Pat. I know it. You don't want to marry the wrong person.''

JOSH

It seemed to Pat that Josh was almost omniscient. *Why should he call when he did? Did he know I have doubts? Maybe it's just last-minute jitters,* he thought.

Pat wrestled with the problem for several days, then three days before the wedding, postponed the marriage.

Six months later, Pat stopped in Dallas to see Josh. Together they went for lunch at a nearby chili shop. Pat grew quite emotional as he recalled their last conversation.

"I can't thank you and the Lord enough for what you did," Pat said. "I called off the wedding...we broke up. Since then God has shown me in many ways it would have been wrong. It wouldn't have had His blessing."

Josh grew suddenly sober and his own eyes began to tear. "There's so much divorce and so many marriages have gone sour," he reflected. "The wrong woman or man can destroy a marriage. I've seen it happen so much. I'm glad it didn't happen to you."

As the seventies turned into the eighties, Josh and Dottie saw new and exciting changes come into their ministry. The team was beginning to absorb a lot of Josh's responsibilities.

Josh was able to spend more time with his family—now increased by two. Sean was born in 1976 and Katie in 1980.

Films, TV specials, books, cassettes, and seminars expanded Josh's outreach to millions. High school, college and university campuses were being reached by other speakers, trained by him.

In order to build a more structured life for his family and spend more time with his children, they moved to a quaint home on the side of a mountain in Julian, California, in March 1980, before Katie was born.

The community had already been settled by several other families, close friends: Dick and Charlotte Day, Paul and Leslie Lewis, and the Simpsons.

Dick Day recalled old times with Josh. "I've seen you grow from a brash, impetuous, driving young man into a sensitive, mature wise man being used of God. It pleases me a great deal that I've been able to watch it and count you as a

CHAPTER
EIGHTEEN

friend.''

"Listen, buddy," Josh said, his arm around his friend. "You know, Barnabas never wrote any letters to churches or books of the Bible...no epistles...there's no 'gospel of Barnabas.' But his role in helping the apostle Paul is very real. That's you to me, brother. Without you, I'd be nothing. I owe you, Dick. I owe you...."

December, 1980, was the first time in 23 *years* that Josh was in his own home for Christmas. It was a very emotional and relaxing experience. Josh went out to the mountain forest and picked out a pine tree. He cut down his own Christmas tree—the first time ever.

It may have been a small thing to someone else. To Josh, cutting down his own Christmas tree, bringing it home, and decorating it with Dottie and the children was an experience that caused him unexpected joy.

When the decorations were in place, they drove to a nearby home where the handful of his friends had gathered. Their little children were dressed up as angels, wise men and shepherds. Little Katie was "baby Jesus" for their manger play. Real animals were used—a donkey, two sheep and a goat. It was held in an old Western barn. The youngsters re-created the Christmas story as older children read from the Bible. After prayer and carols, they enjoyed each other's company—along with hot chocolate and cookies. Josh looked at his wife, his children, and friends and was overcome by the warm emotions of traditions never before experienced, and he wept with happiness.

Have You Heard of the Four Spiritual Laws?

Just as there are physical laws that govern the physical universe, so are there spiritual laws which govern your relationship with God.

LAW ONE

GOD **LOVES** YOU, AND OFFERS A WONDERFUL **PLAN** FOR YOUR LIFE.

(References should be read in context from the Bible wherever possible.)

God's Love

"For God so loved the world, that He gave His only begotten Son, that whoever believes in Him should not perish, but have eternal life" (John 3:16).

God's Plan

(Christ speaking) "I came that they might have life, and might have it abundantly" (that it might be full and meaningful) (John 10:10).

Why is it that most people are not experiencing the abundant life?

Because . . .

LAW TWO

MAN IS **SINFUL** and **SEPARATED** FROM GOD. THEREFORE, HE CANNOT KNOW AND EXPERIENCE GOD'S LOVE AND PLAN FOR HIS LIFE.

Man Is Sinful

"For all have sinned and fall short of the glory of God" (Romans 3:23).

Man was created to have fellowship with God; but, because of his stubborn self-will, he chose to go his own independent way and fellowship with God was broken. This self-will, characterized by an attitude of active rebellion or passive indifference, is evidence of what the Bible calls sin.

Man Is Separated

"For the wages of sin is death" (spiritual separation from God) (Romans 6:23).

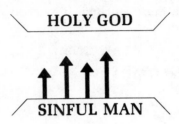

This diagram illustrates that God is holy and man is sinful. A great gulf separates the two. The arrows illustrate that man is continually trying to reach God and the abundant life through his own efforts, such as a good life, philosophy or religion.

The third law explains the only way to bridge this gulf . . .

LAW THREE

JESUS CHRIST IS GOD'S **ONLY** PROVISION FOR MAN'S SIN. THROUGH HIM YOU CAN KNOW AND EXPERIENCE GOD'S LOVE AND PLAN FOR YOUR LIFE.

He Died in Our Place

"But God demonstrates His own love toward us, in that while we were yet sinners, Christ died for us" (Romans 5:8).

He Rose from the Dead

"Christ died for our sins . . . He was buried . . . He was raised on the third day, according to the Scriptures . . . He appeared to Peter, then to the twelve. After that He appeared to more than five hundred . . ." (I Corinthians 15:3-6).

He Is the Only Way to God

"Jesus said to him, 'I am the way, and the truth, and the life; no one comes to the Father, but through Me' " (John 14:6).

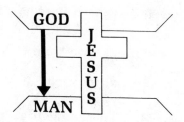

This diagram illustrates that God has bridged the gulf which separates us from God by sending His Son, Jesus Christ, to die on the cross in our place to pay the penalty for our sins.

It is not enough just to know these three laws . . .

LAW FOUR

WE MUST INDIVIDUALLY **RECEIVE** JESUS CHRIST AS SAVIOR AND LORD; THEN WE CAN KNOW AND EXPERIENCE GOD'S LOVE AND PLAN FOR OUR LIVES.

We Must Receive Christ

"But as many as received Him, to them He gave the right to become children of God, even to those who believe in His name" (John 1:12).

We Receive Christ through Faith

"For by grace you have been saved through faith; and that not of yourselves, it is the gift of God; not as a result of works, that no one should boast" (Ephesians 2:8,9).

When We Receive Christ, We Experience a New Birth

(Read John 3:1-8).

We Receive Christ by Personal Invitation

(Christ is speaking) "Behold, I stand at the door and knock; if any one hears My voice and opens the door, I will come in to him" (Revelation 3:20).

Receiving Christ involves turning from self to God (repentance) and trusting Christ to come into our lives to forgive our sins and to make us the kind of person He wants us to be. Just to agree intellectually that Jesus Christ is the Son of God and that He died on the cross for our sins is not enough. Nor is it enough to have an emotional experience. We receive Jesus Christ by faith, as an act of the will.

These two circles represent two kinds of lives:

SELF-DIRECTED LIFE
S—Self on the throne
†—Christ is outside the life
•—Interests are directed by self, often resulting in discord and frustration

CHRIST-DIRECTED LIFE
†—Christ is in the life
S—Self is yielding to Christ
•—Interests are directed by Christ, resulting in harmony with God's plan

Which circle best represents your life?

Which circle would you like to have represent your life?

The following explains how you can receive Christ:

YOU CAN RECEIVE CHRIST RIGHT NOW BY FAITH THROUGH PRAYER

(Prayer is talking with God)

God knows your heart and is not so concerned with your words as He is with the attitude of your heart. The following is a suggested prayer:

"Lord Jesus, I need You. Thank You for dying on the cross for my sins. I open the door of my life and receive You as my Savior and Lord. Thank You for forgiving my sins and giving me eternal life. Make me the kind of person You want me to be."

Does this prayer express the desire of your heart?

If it does, pray this prayer right now, and Christ will come into your life, as He promised.